I0687990

George Edward Woodberry

Studies in Letters and Life

George Edward Woodberry

Studies in Letters and Life

ISBN/EAN: 9783744709705

Printed in Europe, USA, Canada, Australia, Japan

Cover: Foto ©Thomas Meinert / pixelio.de

More available books at **www.hansebooks.com**

STUDIES IN LETTERS
AND LIFE

BY

GEORGE EDWARD WOODBERRY

BOSTON AND NEW YORK
HOUGHTON, MIFFLIN AND COMPANY
The Riverside Press, Cambridge
1891

PREFACE.

THE following Essays are reprinted from *The Atlantic Monthly* and *The Nation*, with little more revision than was necessary to cover unimportant omissions or to combine, in one or two instances, kindred articles. In the hope that they may afford some illustration, however fragmentary and intermittent, of the love of letters and of interest in ideal living, the author offers them to the reader.

BEVERLY, *July* 12, 1890.

CONTENTS.

CRITICISMS.

LANDOR.

MANY of the most sensitive and discriminating critics of this century have, in the suffrage for fame, listed themselves for Landor. He seemed almost to achieve immortality within his lifetime, so continuously was the subtle appreciation of the best yielded to him, from the far-off years when Shelley used, at Oxford, to declaim with enthusiasm passages from Gebir, to the time, that seems as yesterday, when Swinburne made his pilgrimage to Italy, to offer his tribute of adoration to the old man at the close of his solitary and troubled career; and still each finer spirit,

> " As he passes, turns,
> And bids fair peace be to his sable shroud."

During his long life he saw the springtime, and outlived the harvest, of the great poetic revival, and the labor of the Victorian poets of the aftermath was half accomplished before his death; but from all these powerful contemporary influences he was free. He remained apart; and this single fact, attesting, as it does, extraordinary self-possession and assurance of purpose, suffices to make his character interesting, even were his work of inferior worth. As yet, however, even to the minds of cultivated men, he is hardly more than a great figure. He is known, praised, and remembered for particular scenes, dramatic fragments, occasional lyrics, quatrains. This is the natural fate of a discursive writer. It matters not that Landor was wide ranging; it matters not what spoils of thought, what images of beauty, he brought from those far eastern uplands which it was his boast to haunt: he failed to give unity to his work, to give interest to large portions of it, to command public attention for it as a whole. Indeed, his work as a whole does not command the attention even of the best. What does survive, too, lives only in the favor of a small circle. He forfeited popular fame at the beginning, when he selected themes that presuppose rare qualities in his audience, and adopted an antique style; but such considerations, at least in their naked statement, do not tell the whole story. Other poets have missed immediate applause by dealing with subjects that assumed unusual largeness of soul, range of sympathy, and refinement of taste in their readers: like Shelley, singing of unheeded hopes and fears to which the world was to be wrought; like Wordsworth, narrating the myth of Troy. Other poets, in style, have set forth the object plainly, and left it to work its will on the heart and imagination, unaided by the romantic spell, the awakening glow, the silent but imperative suggestion, the overmastering passion that takes heart and imagination captive; and they have not lost their reward. A remote theme, an impersonal style, are not of themselves able to condemn a poet to long neglect. They may make wide appreciation of him impossible; they may explain the indifference of an imperfectly educated public; but they do not account for the fact that Landor is to be read, even by his admirers, in a book of selections, while the dust is shaken from the eight stout octavos that contain his works only by the professional man of letters.

What first strikes the student of Landor

is the lack of any development in his genius. This is one reason why Mr. Leslie Stephen, seizing on the characteristic somewhat rudely, and leaping to an ungracious conclusion, calls him " a glorified and sublime edition of the sixth-form schoolboy." Men whose genius is of this fixed type are rare in English literature, and not of the highest rank. They exhibit no radical change; they are at the beginning what they are at the end; their works do not belong to any particular period of their lives; they seem free from their age, and to live outside of it. Hence, in dealing with them, historical criticism — the criticism whose purpose is to explain rather than to judge — soon finds itself at fault. When the circumstances that determined the original bent of their minds have been set forth, there is nothing more to be said. With Landor, this bent seems to have been given by his classical training. To write Latin verses was the earliest serious employment of his genius, and his efforts were immediately crowned with success. These studies, falling in with natural inclinations and aptitudes, pledged him to a classical manner; they made real for him the myths and history of Greece and Rome;

they fed his devotion to the ancient virtues,
— love of freedom, aspiration for the calm
of wisdom, reverence for the dignity of heroism, delight in beauty for its own sake;
they supported him in what was more distinctively his own, — his refinement in material
tastes, his burning indignation, his defense
of tyrannicide. These characteristics he had
in youth; they were neither diminished nor
increased in age. In youth, too, he displayed
all his literary excellences and defects: the
fullness and weight of line; the march of
sentences; the obscurity arising from over-
condensation of thought and abrupt and el-
liptical constructions; his command of the
grand and impressive as well as the beautiful and charming in imagery; his fondness
for heroic situation and for the loveliness of
minute objects. This was a high endowment; why, then, do its literary results seem
inadequate?

With all his gifts, Landor did not possess
unifying power. He observed objects as
they passed before him at hap-hazard, took
them into his mind, and gave them back, un-
transformed, in their original disorder. He
thought disconnectedly, and expressed his
thoughts as they came, detached and sepa-

rate. This lack of unity did not result simply from his choice of the classical mode of treatment, or from a defect in logical or constructive power, although it was connected with these. The ability to fuse experience, to combine its elements and make them one, to give it back to the world, transformed, and yet essentially true, the real creative faculty, is proportioned very strictly to the self-assertive power of genius, to the energy of the reaction of the mind on nature and life; it springs from a strong personality. To say that Landor's personality was weak would be to stultify one's self; but yet the difference between Landor the man and Landor the author is so great as to make the two almost antithetical; and in his imaginative work, by which he must be judged, it is not too much to say that he denied and forswore his personality, and obliterated himself so far as was possible. He not only eliminated self from his style, and, after the classical manner, defined by Arnold, " relied solely on the weight and force of that which, with entire fidelity, he uttered," but he also eliminated self, so far as one can, from his subject. He did not bind his work together by the laws of his own mind; he did not root it in the truth, as he saw truth; he did not interpenetrate and permeate it with his own beliefs, as the great masters have always done. His principles were at the best vague, hardly amounting to more than an unapplied enthusiasm for liberty, heroism, and the other great watchwords of social rather than individual life. These illuminate his work, but they do not give it consistency. It is crystalline in structure, beautiful, ordered, perfect in form when taken part by part, but conglomerate as a whole; it is a handful of jewels, many of which are singly of the most transparent and glowing light, but unrelated one to another,—placed in juxtaposition, but not set; and in the crystalline mass is imbedded grosser matter, and mingled with the jewels are stones of dull color and light weight. A lovely object caught his eye, and he set it forth in verse; a fine thought came to him, and he inserted it in his dialogues; but his days were not "bound each to each by natural piety," or by any other of the shaping principles of high genius. He was a spectator of life, not an actor in life. Nature was to him a panorama, wonderful, awful, beautiful, and he described its scenes down to its most minute and evanescent details. History was his theatre, where the personages played great parts; and he recorded their words and gestures, always helping them with the device of the high buskin and something of a histrionic air. He was content to be thus guided from without; to have his intellectual activity determined by the chance of sensation and of reading, rather than by a well-thought-out and enthusiastic purpose of his own soul. And so he became hardly more than a mirror of beauty and an Æolian harp of thought; if the vision came, if the wind breathed, he responded.

This self-effacement, this impersonality, as it is called, in literature, is much praised. It is said to be classical, and there is an impression in some minds that such an abdication of the individual's prerogatives is the distinctive mark of classicism. There is no more misleading and confusing error in criticism. Not impersonality, but universality, is that mark; and this is by no means the same thing, differently stated. In any age, the first, although not the sole, characteristic of classical work is that it deals with universal truth, of interest to all men: and hence the poet is required to keep to himself his idiosyncrasies, hobbies, all that is simply his own ; all that is not identical with the common human nature ; all that men in large bodies cannot sympathize with, understand, and appreciate. Under these conditions direct self-revelation is exceptional. The poet usually expresses himself by so arranging his plot and developing his characters that they will illustrate the laws of life, as he sees these laws, without any direct statement, — though the Greek chorus is full of didactic sayings ; and he may also express himself by such a powerful presentation of the morality intrinsic in beautiful things and noble actions as "to soothe the cares and lift the thoughts of men," without any dogmatic insistence in his own person. In these ways Æschylus obliterated himself from his work just as much as Shakespeare, and no more; Swift just as much as Aristophanes, and no more; but the statement that Shakespeare or Swift obliterated themselves from their works needs only to be made to be laughed at. The faith of Æschylus, the wisdom of Sophocles, are in all their dramas; Anacreon is in all his songs, Horace in all his odes. The lasting significance of their productions to mankind is derived from the clearness, the power, the skill, with which they informed their works with their personality. These men had a philosophy of life, that underlay and unified their work. They rebuilt the world in their imagination, and gave it the laws of their own minds. Their spirits were active, moulding, shaping, creating, subduing the whole of nature and life to themselves. It is true that the ancients accomplished their purpose rather by thought, the moderns rather by emotion; but this difference is incidental to the change in civilization. Either instrument is sufficient for its end; but he who would now choose the ancient instead of the modern mode, narrows, postpones, and abbreviates his fame only less than Landor, in his youth, by writing in Latin. Whatever be the mode of its operation, the energy of personality is the very essence of effective genius.

That Landor had no philosophy of life, in the same sense as Shakespeare or Æschylus, is plain to any reader. Those who look on art, including poetry, as removed from ordinary human life, who think that its chief service to men lies in affording delight rather than in that quickening 'of the spirit of which delight is only the sign and efflorescence, would consider Landor's lack of this philosophy a virtue. It accounts largely for his failure to interest even the best in the larger part of his work, and especially for the discontinuity of his reflections. These reflections are always his own; and this fact may seem to make against the view that he eliminated self from his productions so far as possible. But the presence of personality in literature as a force, ordering a great whole and giving it laws, is a very different thing from its presence as a mere mouthpiece of opinion. The thoughts may be numerous, varied, wise, noble; they may have all the virtues of truth and grace; but if they are disparate and scattered, if they tend nowhither, if they leave the reader where they found him, if they subserve no ulterior purpose and accomplish no end, there is a wide gulf between them and the thoughts of Shakespeare and Æschylus, no less their own than were Landor's his. In the former, personality is a power; in the latter, it is only a voice. In Landor's eight volumes there are more fine thoughts, more wise apothegms, than in any other discursive author's works in English literature; but they do not tell on the mind. They bloom

like flowers in their gardens, but they crown
no achievement. At the end, no cause is
advanced, no goal is won. This incoherence
and inefficiency proceed from the absence of
any definite scheme of life, any compacted
system of thought, any central principles,
any strong, pervading, and ordering personality.

In the same way the objectivity of Landor's work, its naturalism as distinguished
from imaginativeness, results from the same
cause, but with the difference that, while
the faults already mentioned are largely due
to an imperfect equipment of the mind, his
mode of art seems to have been adopted by
conscious choice and of set purpose. The
opinion of those who look on naturalism as
a virtue in art is deserving of respect. We
have been admonished .for a long while that
men should see things as they are, and present them as they are, and that this was the
Greek way. The dictum, when applied
with the meaning that men should be free
from prejudice and impartial in judgment,
no one would contest; but when it is pro-
claimed with the meaning that poets should
express ideas nakedly, and should reproduce
objects by portraiture, there is excuse for

raising some question. No doubt, this was in general the practice of the ancients. The Athenians were primarily intellectual, the Romans unimaginative. But by the operation of various causes — the chief of which are the importance bestowed on the individual and the impulse given to emotion by the Christian religion — mankind has changed somewhat; and therefore the methods of appeal to men, the ways of touching their hearts and enlightening their minds, have been modified. In literature this change is expressed by saying that the romantic manner has, in general, superseded the classical. The romantic manner aims at truth no less than the classical; it sets forth things as they are no less completely and clearly. The difference is rather one of methods than of aims. The classical poet usually perceives the object by his intellect, and makes his appeal to the mind; the romantic poet seizes on the object with his imagination, and makes his appeal to the heart. Not that classical work is without imagination, or romantic work devoid of intellectuality; but that in one the intellect counts for more, in the other imagination. The classical poet, having once presented ideas and objects,

leaves them to make their way; the romantic
poet not only presents them, but, by awakening the feelings, predisposes the mood of the
mind, makes their reception by the mind
easier, wins their way for them. In classical work, consequently, success depends
mainly on lucidity of understanding, clearness of vision, skill in verbal expression ; in
romantic work, the poet must not only possess these qualities, but must superadd, as
his prime characteristic, rightness, one might
better say sanity, of passion. The classical
virtues are more common among authors,
the romantic far more rare; and hence error in the romantic manner is more frequent,
especially in dealing with ideas. But with
all its liability to mistake in weak hands,
romantic art, by its higher range, its fiercer
intensity, especially by its greater certainty,
has, in the hands of a master, a clear increase of power over classical art, and under
the changed conditions of civilization its resources are not to be lightly neglected. Indeed, one who voluntarily adopts the classical manner as an exclusive mode seems to
choose an instrument of less compass and
melody, to prefer Greek to modern music.
He sings to a secluded and narrow circle,

and loses the ear of the world. Certainly Landor made this choice, and by it he must stand.

Let us take an example from the best of Landor's work, and from that region of classical art where it is wholly competent, — the brief description of small objects : —

> "The ever-sacred cup
> Of the pure lily hath between my hands
> Felt safe, unsoiled, nor lost one grain of gold."

How completely, how distinctly, the image is given, — its form, its transparent purity, its fragile and trembling gold! How free from any other than a strictly artistic charm! And yet how different is its method of appeal from Shelley's

> "tender blue-bells, at whose birth
> The sod scarce heaved;"

from Shakespeare's

> "daffodils
> That come before the swallow dares, and take
> The winds of March with beauty."

Or, to select an illustration, also of Landor's best, when the image, no less objective, yields of itself an infinite suggestion : —

> "Borgia, thou once wert almost too august
> And high for adoration; now thou 'rt dust.
> All that remains of thee these plaits unfold,
> Calm hair meandering in pellucid gold."

Again, how perfect is the image, how effective the development of the third line; how the melody of the last blends with its selected epithets to place the object entire and whole before the mind; how free is the quatrain from any self-intrusion of the poet! But here, too, the method of appeal is very different from Shakespeare's, as in the lines on Yorick's skull: "Here hung those lips that I have kissed I know not how oft." The difference in mood between these two only emphasizes the difference in method. Enough has been said, however, in description and exemplification of the two kinds of art. Either is sufficient for its ends, nor would any one desire to dispense with that which has resulted in work so admirable as has been quoted from Landor. The distinctively romantic poets do not consign the classical style to disuse. In the presentation of images, Keats has frequent recourse to it, as in his picture of Autumn lying

> "on a half-reaped furrow sound asleep,
> Drowsed with the fume of poppies, while thy hook
> Spares the next swath and all its twinèd flowers."

So Wordsworth, in expressing ideas, is sometimes more bald than the least imaginative of the classics. But such poets do not

employ this style alone; they are characterized by the modern manner; they give us
those " sweet views " which in the ancient
mode " can never well be seen." Landor
droops below his great contemporaries, not
by merely adopting the classical method,
but by adopting it exclusively. Whether
this choice was entirely free, or partly determined by natural incapacity, is doubtful.
Violent and tempestuous as his nature was,
with all his boyish intensity of indignation,
his boyish delicacy of tenderness, he seems
to possess temper rather than true passion.
In the verses to his poetic love, Ianthe, there
are many fine sentiments, graceful turns;
there is courtliness of behavior; but the
note of passion is not struck. Ianthe is
only another poetic mistress of the cavalier
school, and in the memory her name is less,
both for dignity and pathos, than Rose Aylmer's. Without passion, of course, a poet is
condemned to the classical style. Passion
is the element in which the romantic writer
fuses beauty and wisdom; it is the means
by which personality pervades literary work
with most ease, directness, and glow. In
the great modern poets it is the substance of
their genius. But just as neither by a phi-

losophy of life nor in any other way did
Landor fill his subject with himself, so neither by passion nor by any other quality did
he breathe his own spirit into his style.

The consequence is that Landor, unclassified in his own age, is now to be ranked
among the poets, increasing in number, who
appeal rather to the artistic than to the
poetic sense. He is to be placed in that
group which looks on art as a world removed; which prizes it mainly for the delight it gives; which, caring less for truth,
deals chiefly with the beauty that charms
the senses; and which therefore weaves poetry like tapestry, and uses the web of speech ·
to bring out a succession of fine pictures.
The watchwords of any school, whether in
thought or art, seldom awake hostility until
their bearing on the details of practice reveals their meaning. Art is, in a sense, a
world removed from the actual and present
life, and beauty is the sole title that admits
any work within its limits. Of this there is
no question. But that world, however far
from what is peculiar to any one age, has its
eternal foundations in universal life; and
that beauty has its enduring power because
it is the incarnation of universal life. What

poem has a better right to admission there
than The Eve of St. Agnes? and in what
poem does the heart of life beat more
warmly? Laodamia belongs in that world,
but it is because it voices abiding human
feelings no less than because of its serenity.
Nature in itself is savage, sterile, and void;
individual life in itself is trifling: each obtains its value through its interest to humanity as a whole, and the office of art is to set
forth that value. A lovely object, a noble
action, are each of worth to men, but the
latter is of the more worth; and, as was
long ago pointed out, poetry is by the limitations of language at a considerable disad-
vantage in treating of formal beauty. But
without developing these remarks, of which
there is no need, the only point here to be
made is that in so far as poetry concerns itself with objects without relation to ideas, it
loses influence; in so far as it neglects emotion and thought for the purpose of gaining
sensuous effects it loses worth; in both it
declines from the higher to the lower levels.
Landor, notwithstanding his success in presenting objects of artistic beauty — and his
poetry is full of exquisite delineations of
them — failed to interest men; nor could his

skill in expressing thought, although he was far more intellectual than his successors, save his reputation. Landor mistook a few of the marks of art for all. His work has the serenity, the remoteness, that characterize high art, but it lacks an intimate relation with the general life of men; it sets forth formal beauty, as painting does, but that beauty remains a sensation, and does not pass into thought. This absence of any vital relation between his art and life, between his objects and ideas, denotes his failure. There are so many poets whose works contain as perfect beauty, and in addition truth and passion; so many who instead of mirroring beauty make it the voice of life, — who instead of responding in melodious thought to the wandering winds of reverie strike their lyres in the strophe and antistrophe of continuous song, — that the world is content to let Landor go by. The guests at the famous late dinner-party to which he looked forward will indeed be very few, and they will be men of leisure.

Thus far, in examining the work of Landor as a whole, and endeavoring to understand somewhat the public indifference to it, the answer has been found in its objectivity

and its discontinuity, both springing from
the effacement of his personality as an active power; or, in other words, in the fact
that, by failing to link his images with his
thoughts, and his thoughts one with another,
so as to make them tell on the mind, and
especially by eliminating the romantic element of passion, he failed to bring his work
into sympathetic or helpful relations with
the general emotional and intellectual life of
men.

Why, then, do the most sensitive and
discriminating critics, as was said at the beginning, list themselves in Landor's favor?
They are, without exception, fellow-workers
with him in the craft of literature. They
have, by their continued eulogy of him,
made it a sign of refinement to be charmed
by him, a proof of unusually good taste to
praise him. His admirers, by their very divergence in opinion from the crowd, seem
to claim uncommon sensibilities; and the co-
terie is certainly one of the highest order, intellectually: Browning, Lowell, Swinburne,
to name no more. They are all literary
men. They are loud in their plaudits of his
workmanship, but are noticeably guarded
in their commendation of his entire con-

tents; the passages for which they express unstinted enthusiasm are few. Landor was, beyond doubt, a master-workman, and skill in workmanship is dear to the craft; others may feel its effects, but none appreciate it with the keen relish of the professional author. The fullness, power, and harmony of Landor's language are clearly evident in his earliest work. He had the gift of literary expression from his youth, and in his mature work it shows as careful and high cultivation as such a gift ever received from its possessor. None could give keener point and smoother polish to a short sentence; none could thread the intricacies of long and involved constructions more unerringly. He had at command all the grammatical resources of lucidity, though he did not always care to employ them. He knew all the devices of prose composition to conceal and to disclose; to bring the commonplace to issue in the unexpected; to lead up, to soften, to hesitate, to declaim; to extort all the supplementary and new suggestions of an old comparison; to frame a new and perfect simile; in short, he was thoroughly trained to his art. Yet his prose is not, by present canons, perfect prose. It is not self-possessed, subdued, and graceful conversation, modulated, making its points without aggressive insistence, yet with certainty, keeping interest alive by a brilliant but natural turn and by the brief and luminous flash of truth through a perfect phrase. His prose is rather the monologue of a seer. In reading his works one feels somewhat as if sitting at the feet of Coleridge. Landor has the presence that abashes companions. His manner of speech is more dignified, more ceremonial, his enunciation is more resonant, his accent more exquisite, than belong to the man of the world. He silences his readers by the mere impossibility of interrupting with a question so noble and smooth-sliding a current of words. The style is a sort of modern Miltonic; it has the suggestion of the pulpit divine in Hooker, the touch of formal artificiality that characterizes the first good English prose. Landor goes far afield for his vocables; his page is a trifle too polysyllabic, has too much of the surface glitter of Latinity. But in the age that produced the styles of De Quincey, Ruskin, and Carlyle, it would be mere folly to find fault because Landor did not write, we will not say after the French fashion, but after the fashion of Swift, at

his highest and on his level, the unrivaled
master of simple English prose. Landor, at
his best, is not so picturesque as De Quincey, nor so eloquent as Ruskin, nor so intense as Carlyle ; but he has more self-possession, more serenity, more artistic charm,
a wider compass, a more equal harmony,
than any of these.

Landor pleases his fellow-craftsmen, however, not only by this general command of
language as a means of expression, but by
the perfection of form in his short pieces.
Perfection of form is the great feature of
classical art ; it is an intellectual virtue, at
least in literature, and appeals to the mind.
The moderns are lacking in it. Landor's
command of form was limited, insufficient
for the construction of a drama ; impressive
as Count Julian is, it has not this final excellence. Landor's power in this respect is
analogous to Herrick's ; it is perfect only
within narrow bounds; but it lacks Herrick's spontaneity. His verses are not the
" swallow flights of song ; " he was not a
singer. The lyric on Rose Aylmer is entirely exceptional, and much of its charm lies
in the beauty of the name, the skillful repe-
tition, and, we must add, in the memory of

Lamb's fondness for it. Familiar as it is, it would be unjust not to quote it : —

> " Ah, what avails the sceptred race !
>   Ah, what the form divine !
> What every virtue, every grace !
>   Rose Aylmer, all were thine.
> Rose Aylmer, whom these wakeful eyes
>   May weep, but never see,
> A night of memories and of sighs
>   I consecrate to thee."

Ordinarily, however, Landor deals with a beautiful image or one fine sentiment. His objectivity, his discontinuity, help him here; they insure that simplicity and singleness which are necessary for success. The lack of any temptation in his mind to expound and suggest is probably one reason why he rejected the sonnet, certainly the most beautiful poetic mould to give shape to such detached thoughts and feelings. He scorned the sonnet; it was too long for him; he must be even more brief. He would present the object at once, instead of gradually, as the sonnet does; not unveiling the perfect and naked image until the last word has trembled away. His best work of this kind is in the quatrain, which is rather the moralist's than the poet's form,—Martial's, not Horace's.

> " I strove with none, for none was worth my strife.
>   Nature I loved, and, next to Nature, Art;
> I warmed both hands before the fire of life,
>   It sinks, and I am ready to depart."

This is perfect; but it is perfect speech, not perfect song. When Landor had something to say at more length, when he had a story to tell, he chose the idyl; and his work in this kind is no less perfect in form than are his quatrains. Indeed, on the idyls his poetic fame will mainly rest. They are very remote from modern life, but the best of them are very beautiful, and in the highest rank of poetry that appeals to the artistic sense. Those who are able still to hold fast to the truth of Greek mythology to the imagination will not willingly let them die. To read them is like looking at the youths and maidens of an ancient bas-relief. The cultivated will never tire of them; the people will never care for them. The limitations of their interest are inherent in their subject and the mode of its presentation; but these limitations do not lessen their beauty, although they make very small the number who appreciate it.

Landor's influence over his critics is due chiefly to his power as a stylist, and to the perfection of form in his shorter poems and his idyls; but something is also due to the passages which, apart from those mentioned, they commend so unreservedly; such as the study of incipent insanity in the dialogue between Tiberius and Vipsania, and the scenes from Antony and Octavius where the boy Cæsarion is an actor. Not to be conquered by these argues one's self "dull of soul;" and scattered through the volumes are other passages of only less mastery, especially in the Greek dialogues, which cannot here be particularized. For this reason no author is more served than Landor by a book of selections. After all, too, an author should be judged by his best. Nevertheless, when one remembers the extraordinary gifts of Landor, one cannot but regret the defects of nature and judgment that have so seriously interfered with his influence. His work as a whole exhibits a sadder waste of genius than is the case even with Coleridge. There is no reason to suppose that the verdict of the public on his value will be reversed. His failure may well serve as a warning to the artistic school in poetry; it affords one more of the long list of illustrations of that fundamental truth in literature,—the truth that a man's work is of service to mankind in proportion as, by expressing himself in it, by filling it with his own personality, he fills it with human interest.

CRABBE.

WE have done with Crabbe. His tales have failed to interest us. Burke and his friends, as we all know, held a different opinion from ours; and their praise is not likely to have been ill founded. The cultivated taste of Holland House, thirty years later, is also against our decision. Through two generations of markedly different literary temper Crabbe pleased the men best worth pleasing. Indeed, we owe him to Burke's approval; for when Lord North, Lord Shelburne, and Lord Thurlow had neglected his entreaties for recognition and aid, and had left him to write, pawn, and go hungry, Burke saved him from the debtor's prison, took him into his friendship, welcomed him to his home, and gave him to literature.

Yet the verses which won this recognition from Burke, and gained for Crabbe, besides, praise from Johnson and talk with Fox and idle mornings in Reynolds's studio, were only his fledgeling flights. It was not until after more than twenty years of silence, spent in the obscurity of a country clergyman's life, that he showed the richness and abundance of his vein. Then Burke and his friends had given place to those younger men, in whose lives a new age was dawning; but as warm a welcome awaited Crabbe among them as he had ever met with in Burke's club. With them he passed his old age, pleased with Byron's praise, and with the friendliness of Moore and Rogers, and with Scott's kindly regard and correspondence. They liked to see him, with his beautiful white hair, his formal, old - fashioned garb and old-school manners, the last of that long line of poets through whom the Queen Anne taste had tyrannized for a century in English verse, sitting familiarly among themselves, who were preparing the way for the next generation to ignore the traditions which Burke and Johnson had fixed in his poetic faith. Especially did Sir Walter honor him; like Fox, he chose Crabbe's poems to be read to him just before he died.

Without reckoning the approval of others, what was the strong attraction in Crabbe's work for Scott and Fox? Their judgment was not so worthless that it can be disregarded with the complacent assurance with which the decisions of Gifford and Jeffrey are set aside; on the contrary, Scott had such health and Fox such refinement that their judgment ought to raise a doubt whether our generation is not making a mistake and missing pleasure through its neglect of Crabbe.

Crabbe is a story-teller. He describes the life he saw, — common, homely life, sometimes wretched, not infrequently criminal; the life of the country poor, with occasional light and shadow from the life of the gentlefolk above them. He had been born into it, in a village on the Suffolk coast, amid stern and cheerless natural scenes : landward, the bramble-overgrown heath encompassing crowded and mean houses; eastward, —

"Stakes and sea-weed withering on the mud."

Here he had passed his boyhood, in the midst of human life equally barren and stricken with the ugliness of poverty, among surly and sordid fishers given to hard labor and rough brawl, —

"A joyless, wild, amphibious race,
With sullen woe displayed in every face," —

and the sight had been a burden to him. The desire to throw off this twofold oppression of mean nature and humanity must have counted for much in determining him on that long - remembered December day, when, as the bleak twilight came down, darkening the marshy pool on the heath where he stood, he took his resolve to go up to London and seek poetical fame; and glad at heart he must have been, that morning of early spring, when he left all this ugliness behind him, ignorant of the struggle and distress he was to meet where he was going.

In that early poem which Johnson praised Crabbe described this village life with the vigor of a youth who had escaped out of its dreary imprisonment, and without a touch of that tenderness for early associations which softened Goldsmith's retrospect of the scenes of his early days. Crabbe told of exhausting labor leading on to prematurely useless and neglected age; of storms sweeping away the shelter of the poor; of smugglers, poachers, wreckers, tavern debauchery, and, worst of all, the poor-house — a terrible picture, perhaps the best known of all his drawing — with its deserted inmates cut off from all human care except that of the heedless phy-

sician and the heartless parson; a miserable
tale, but too much of it only what his own
eyes had seen. We do not know the contents of those piles of manuscripts which he
wrote during his twenty years of silence,
and — not much to the world's loss, some
think — made bonfires of to amuse his children; but his first poem after that long interval was the same story, the experience of
those whose names appeared in the year's
parish register of births, marriages, and
deaths, and was a sorrowful survey of seduction, desertion, crime, discontent, and folly.
In his later tales he dealt less in unrelieved
gloom and bitter misery, and at times made
a trial at humor. There are glimpses of pleasant English life and character, but these
are only glimpses; the ground of his painting
is shadow, — the shadow that rested on the
life of the English poor in his generation.

Where else would one turn for an adequate description of that life, or gain so direct an insight into the social sources and
conditions of the Methodist revival, or into
the motives and convictions of reformers
like Mary Wollstonecraft? Where would
one obtain so keen a sense of the vast change
which has taken place in the conditions of

humble human life within this century?
Mr. Leslie Stephen, in that essay which is
so good-humored but .so unsuccessful an attempt to appreciate Crabbe, mentions the
few illustrations in modern literature of the
life Crabbe described; it is seen in Char-
lotte Brontë's Yorkshiremen, and George
Eliot's millers, and in a few other characters, " but," he says, " to get a realistic picture of country life as Crabbe saw it, we
must go back to Squire Western, or to some
of the roughly-hewn masses of flesh who
sat to Hogarth." The setting of Crabbe's
tales has this special historic interest. The
schools, houses, books, habits, occupations, .
and all the external characteristics of the
tales belong to the time: the press-gang
comes to carry off the lover just before his
wedding-day, and leaves the bride to nurse
an unfathered child, to receive the courtship
of a canting and carnal preacher, and to find
a refuge from him, and from the father who
favors him, in suicide; orphan boys are
bound over to brutal task-masters; pictures
of the sects (from the pen of a respectable
clergyman of the Established Church, it is
true) recall the beginnings of Methodism
with a vividness only to be equaled by the

books and pamphlets of the early converts'
own writing. This historic value of the
tales, however, great as it is to the student
of manners, is secondary to their poetic
value, which lies in the sentiment, feeling,
and pathos with which the experience of life
embodied in·them, the workings of simple
human nature, in however debased surroundings, is set forth. It is an experience which
results usually from the interplay of low and
selfish motives, and of ignoble or weak passions ; it is, too often, the course of brutal
appetite, thoughtless or heartless folly, avarice, sensuality, and vice, relieved too seldom
by amiable character, sympathy, charity,
self-sacrifice, or even by the charm of natural beauty. Yet if all the seventy tales
be taken into account, they contain nearly
all varieties of character and circumstance
among the country poor ; and, though the
darker side may seem to be more frequently
insisted upon, it is because the nature of his
subject made it necessary, because he let his
light, as Moore said, —

> "Through life's low, dark interior fall,
>   Opening the whole, severely bright,"

rather than because he had any lack of
cheerfulness of temper.

Crabbe does not, in a true sense, give expression to the life of the poor ; he merely narrates it. Here and there, throughout the poems, are episodes written out of his own life ; but usually he is concerned with the experience of other men, which he had observed, rather than with what his own heart had felt. A description of life is of course far inferior to an utterance of it, such as was given to us by Burns, who dealt with the life of the poor so much more powerfully than Crabbe ; and a realistic description has less poetic value than an imaginative one, such as was given to us by Wordsworth at his best. Crabbe's description is perhaps the most nakedly realistic of any in English poetry ; but it is an uncommonly good one. Realism has a narrow compass, and Crabbe's powers were confined strictly within it ; but he had the best virtues of a realist. His physical vision — his sight of what presents itself to the eye — was almost perfect ; he saw every object, and saw it as it was. Perhaps the minuteness with which he saw was not altogether an advantage, for he does not seem to have taken in the landscape as a whole, but only as a mosaic of separate objects. He never gives general effects of beauty or grandeur; indeed, he seldom saw the beauty of a single object; he did little more than catalogue the things before him, and employ in writing poetry the same faculty in the same way as in pursuing his favorite studies of botany and entomology. Yet, with these limitations, what realist in painting could exceed in truthfulness and carefulness of detail this picture of a fall morning? —

" It was a fair and mild autumnal sky,
  And earth's ripe treasures met th' admiring eye;
  The wet and heavy grass where feet had strayed,
  Not yet erect, the wanderer's way betrayed;
  Showers of the night had swelled the deep'ning rill,
  The morning breeze had urged the quick'ning mill;
  Long yellow leaves, from osiers strewed around,
  Choked the small stream and hushed the feeble sound."

Or this sketch of light in a decayed warehouse turned into a tenement for the poor? —

" That window view! oiled paper and old glass
  Stain the strong rays, which, though impeded, pass,
  And give a dusty warmth to that huge room,
  The conquered sunshine's melancholy gloom;
  When all those western rays, without so bright,
  Within become a ghastly glimmering light,
  As pale and faint upon the floor they fall,
  Or feebly gleam on the opposing wall."

Nor is this carefulness of detail a trick, such as is sometimes employed, to give the ap-

pearance of reality to unreal human life.
Crabbe's mental vision, his sight into the
workings of the passions and the feelings,
although not so perfect as his physical vision, was yet at its best very keen and clear;
the sentiments, moods, reflections, and actions of his characters are seldom contrary
to nature. It would be difficult to show a
finer delineation of its kind than his description of the meeting of two long-parted brothers. As Richard approaches his brother's
hall, he reflects, —

> "'How shall I now my unknown way explore, —
> He proud and rich, I very proud and poor?
> Perhaps my friend a dubious speech mistook,
> And George may meet me with a stranger's look.
> How stands the case? My brother's friend and mine
> Met at an inn, and set them down to dine;
> When, having settled all their own affairs,
> And kindly canvassed such as were not theirs,
> Just as my friend was going to retire,
> "Stay! you will see the brother of our squire,"
> Said his companion; "be his friend, and tell
> The captain that his brother loves him well,
> And when he has no better thing in view
> Will be rejoiced to see him. Now, adieu!"
>
> "'Well, here I am; and, brother, take you heed,
> I am not come to flatter you and feed.
> You shall no soother, fawner, hearer, find;
> I will not brush your coat, nor smooth your mind;
> I will not hear your tales the whole day long,

Nor swear you' re right, if I believe you wrong;
I will not earn my dinner when I dine
By taking all your sentiments for mine;
Nor watch the guiding motions of your eye
Before I venture question or reply.
Yet, son of that dear mother could I meet —
But lo! the mansion, — 't is a fine old seat! '

" The brothers met, with both too much at heart
To be observant of each other's part.
'Brother, I 'm glad! ' was all that George could say,
Then stretched his hand, and turned his head away;
Richard, meantime, made some attempt to speak,
Strong in his purpose, in his trial weak.
At length, affection, like a risen tide,
Stood still, and then seemed slowly to subside;
Each on the other's looks had power to dwell,
And brother brother greeted passing well."

These qualities of fine, true physical and mental vision are the essential qualities for valuable realistic work; if there be room for regret in Crabbe's share of them, it is because their range is contracted. The limitations of his physical vision have been mentioned; in respect to his mental vision Crabbe saw only a few and comparatively simple operations of human nature, — the workings of country-bred minds, not finely or complexly organized, but slow-motioned, and perplexed, if perplexed at all, not from the difficulty of the problem, but from their own dullness. Yet within these limits his characters are often pathetic, sometimes tragic, or even terrible, in their energy of evil passion or remorse.

One other quality, without which clear mental and physical vision would be ineffective, is essential to realism like Crabbe's, — transparency, the quality by virtue of which life is seen through the text plainly and without distortion; and this is the quality which Crabbe possessed in most perfection. He not only saw the object as it was: he presented it as it was. He neither added nor took away; he did not unconsciously darken or heighten color, soften or harden line. Whatever was before his mind — the conversation of a gossip, the brutality of a ruffian, the cant of a convert — he reproduced truthfully; whatever was the character of his story, mean or tragic, trivial or pathetic, he did not modify it. There was no veil of fancy, no glamour of amiable deception or dimness of charitable tears, to obscure his view: if he found nudity and dirt, they reappeared in his work nudity and dirt still; if he found courage and patience, he dealt the same even-handed justice. His distinction is that he told a true story.

It was, perhaps, because he was thus able

to present accurately and faithfully the human life which he saw so clearly that he won such admiration from Scott; for Scott had the welcome of genius for any new glimpse of humanity, and he knew how rare, and consequently how valuable, is the gift of simple and direct narration of what one sees. Fox had great sensibility and tenderness of heart; and Crabbe presented the lot of the poor so vividly, so lucidly, so immediately, that he stirred in Fox the same feelings with which a better poet would have so charged his verses that natures not so finely endowed as Fox would have been compelled to feel them too. Scott and Fox knew what a valuable acquisition this realistic sketch of humble life in their generation was, so faithful, minute, and trustworthy; they felt that their experience was enlarged, that real humanity had been brought home to them, and in the sway of those emotions, which Crabbe did not infuse into his work, but which his work quickens in sympathetic hearts, they could forgive him his tediousness, his frequent commonplace, his not unusual absurdity of phrase, his low level of flight with its occasional feebleness of wing.

In their minds, too, his style must have

had more influence than we are apt to think,
— the style of the great school which died
with him, the form and versification which
they had been taught to believe almost essential to the best poetry, and from a traditional respect for which they could hardly
free their minds as easily as ourselves.
Crabbe used the old heroic rhymed couplet,
that simplest form of English verse music,
which could rise, nevertheless, to the almost
lyric loftiness of the last lines of the Dun-
ciad ; so supple and flexible ; made for easy
simile and compact metaphor ; lending itself
so perfectly to the sudden flash of wit or
turn of humor ; the natural shell of an epi-
gram ; compelling the poet to practice all
the virtues of brevity ; checking the wandering fancy, and repressing the secondary
thought ; requiring in a masterly use of it
the employment of more mental powers than
any other metrical form ; despised and neglected now because the literature which is
embodied in it is despised and neglected, yet
the best metrical form which intelligence, as
distinct from poetical feeling, can employ.
Crabbe did not handle it in any masterful
way ; he was careless, and sometimes slip-
shod ; but when he chose he could employ it

well, and should have credit for it. To take
one more example from his poems, how ex-
cellently he uses it in this passage! —

> " Where is that virtue which the generous boy
>   Felt, and resolved that nothing should destroy;
>   He who with noble indignation glowed
>   When vice had triumph; who his tear bestowed
>   On injured merit? He who would possess
>   Power, but to aid the children of distress!
>   Who has such joy in generous actions shown,
>   And so sincere they might be called his own;
>   Knight, hero, patriot, martyr! on whose tongue
>   And potent arm a nation's welfare hung, —
>   Where now this virtue's fervor, spirit, zeal?
>   Who felt so warmly, has he ceased to feel?
>   Or are these feelings varied? Has the knight,
>   Virtue's own champion, now refused to fight?
>   Is the deliverer turned th' oppressor now?
>   Has the reformer dropt the dangerous vow?
>   Or has the patriot's bosom lost its heat,
>   And forced him, shivering, to a snug retreat?
>   Is such the grievous lapse of human pride!
>   Is such the victory of the worth untried! "

Scott felt an attraction in such poetic form
which we have perhaps ceased to feel; and
Fox, had he lived to read it, would equally
have acknowledged its power.

But Wordsworth said Crabbe was unpoetical; he condemned him for "his unpoetical mode of considering human nature and
society;" and, after all, the world has agreed
with Wordsworth, and disagreed with Scott

and Fox. Wordsworth told Scott an anecdote in illustration of his meaning. Sir
George Beaumont, sitting with himself and
Crabbe one day, blew out the candle which
he had used in sealing a letter. Sir George
and Wordsworth, with proper taste, sat
watching the smoke rise from the wick in
beautiful curves; but Crabbe seeing — or
rather smelling — the object, and not seeing
the beauty of it, put on the extinguisher.
Therefore, said Wordsworth, Crabbe is unpoetical, — as fine a bit of æsthetic priggish-
ness as is often met with. Scott's opinion
was not much affected by the anecdote, and
Wordsworth was on the wrong track. It
is true, however, that Crabbe was unpoetical in Wordsworth's sense. Crabbe had no
imaginative vision, — no such vision as is
shown in that stormy landscape of Shelley's,
in the opening of The Revolt of Islam, which
lacks the truth of actuality, but possesses
the higher imaginative truth, like Turner's
painting, or as is shown in that other storm
in Pippa Passes. Crabbe saw sword-grass
and saltwort and fen, but he had no secret
of the imagination by which he could mingle them into harmonious beauty; there is
loveliness in a salt marsh, but Crabbe could

not present it, nor even see it for himself.
As in landscape so in life. Goldsmith was
untrue to the actual Auburn, but he was
faithful to a far more precious truth, the
truth of remembered childhood, and he revealed with the utmost beauty the effect of
the subtlest working of the spirit of man on
practical fact; it is his fidelity to this psychological and spiritual truth which makes
Auburn the "loveliest village of the plain."
Crabbe exhibited nothing of this imaginative transformation of the familiar -and the
commonplace, perhaps saw nothing of it; he
described the fishing village of Aldborough
as any one with good powers of perception,
who took the trouble, might see it. Through
these defects of his powers he loses in poetic
value; his poetry is, as he called it, poetry
without an atmosphere; it is a reflection,
almost mirror-like, of plain fact.

Men go to poetry too often with a preconceived notion of what the poet ought to
give, instead of with open minds for whatever he has to give. Too much is not to be
expected from Crabbe. He was only a simple country clergyman, half educated, with
no burning ideals, no reveries, no passionate dreams; his mind did not rise out of

the capabilities and virtues of respectability.
His life was as little poetical, in Wordsworth's sense, as his poetry. Yet his gift
was not an empty one. Moore, Scott, and
Byron were story-tellers who were poetical,
in Wordsworth's sense ; but is Crabbe's true
description of humble life less valuable than
Scott's romantic tradition, or Moore's melt-
ing, senuous Oriental dream, or Byron's sentimental, falsely-heroic adventure ? It is far
more valuable, because there is more of the
human heart in it ; because it contains actual
suffering and joy of fellow-men ; because it
is humanity, and calls for hospitality in our
sympathies and charities. Unpoetical? Yes ;
but it is something to have real life brought
home to our tears and laughter, although it
be presented barely, and the poet has trusted
to the rightness and tenderness of our hearts
for those feelings the absence of which in
his verse led Wordsworth to call these tales
unpoetical. But it is only when Crabbe is
at his best that his verse has this extraordinary power.

ON THE PROMISE OF KEATS.

In the domestic, chatty, and nonsense portions of the letters of Keats, in their chaff-
ing, their abandon, their unregarded laughter (and admirable fooling they are, too),
there is a spontaneous and irresponsible
gayety, which, being quite natural only to
the young heart and mind, charmingly dis-
closes his youthfulness as a prime quality.
Of all the famous English poets, he had most
of the spirit of April in him. His senses
were keen; his temperament was feverish,
now jealous and irritable, and straightway
humble and indulgent; his imaginary joys
and sorrows were spiritual possessions, sub-
jecting him; his humor was scampering,
his fancy teeming, his taste erratic, his critical faculty exposed to balking enthusiasms;
his opinions of men and affairs were hasty,
circumscribed, frequently adopted unreflect-
ingly at second-hand; and, with all these boyish traits, he was extremely self-absorbed.
At the centre of his individuality, never-

theless, was the elemental spark, the saving power of genius, the temperance, sanity, and self-reverence of a fine nature gradually coming to the knowledge of its faculties and unriddling the secret of its own moral beauty. Hence Lord Houghton, doing more essential justice to Keats than any of his louder eulogists, describes his works as rather the exercises of his poetical education than the charactery of his original and free power; and Matthew Arnold, even when placing him with Shakespeare, excuses him as a 'prentice hand in the wisest art. Too many of his admirers, seizing upon the external, accidental, and temporal in his biography and the fragmentary and parasitical in his poetry, have really wronged Keats more than did the now infamous reviews; they have rescued him from among the cockneys only to confound him with the neo-pagans. In what did the promise of Keats lie? The first step in the inquiry is the recognition of his immaturity, — the acknowledgment that his memorials must be searched for the germ rather than the fruit.

Sensuous Keats was, as every poet whose inspiration is direct from Heaven must be; unfortunately, the extraordinary beauty and facility of his descriptions of sensation, and his taste for climax and point in his prose have made it easy to quote phrases which seem to show that he was unduly attached to delights of mere sense. To pass by the anecdotes of Haydon, not too scrupulous a truth-teller, here is a characteristic paragraph written to his brother George:—

"This morning I am in a sort of temper, indolent, and supremely careless; I long after a stanza or two of Thomson's Castle of Indolence; my passions are all asleep, from my having slumbered till nearly eleven, and weakened the animal fibre all over me to a delightful sensation about three degrees this side of faintness. If I had teeth of pearl and the breath of lilies, I should call it languor; but as I am I must call it laziness. In this state of effeminacy, the fibres of the brain are relaxed in common with the rest of the body, and to such a happy degree that pleasure has no show of enticement and pain no unbearable frown; neither poetry, nor ambition, nor love have any alertness of countenance; as they pass by me, they seem rather like three figures in a Greek vase, two men and a woman, whom no one but myself could distinguish in their disguise-

ment.   This is the only happiness, and is a
rare instance of advantage in the body overpowering the mind."

With similiar zest he enumerates the
pleasures of drinking claret or of eating a
peach, or he describes his " East Indian "
to his brother's wife : " She kept me awake
one night, as a tune of Mozart's might do.
I speak of the thing as a pastime and an
amusement, than which I can feel none
deeper than a conversation with an imperial
woman, the very 'yes' and 'no' of whose
lips is to me a banquet. . . .   As a man of
the world, I love the rich talk of a Char-
mian; as an eternal being, I love the thought
of you.   I should like her to ruin me, and I
should like you to save me."

Such quick susceptibility to sensuous impressions of every kind may be plentifully
illustrated by opening almost at random in
his works. But the characteristics that mark
the real sensualist — the content that the
lotus-leaf vapors forth, the fierceness of the
centaur's pursuit, the struggle of the faun's
transformation — are nowhere to be found
in the letters or the poems ; before his illness, at least, there is no debility, irresolu-
tion, or mastery of the instincts over the

mind. In fact, without any revolution of his nature, without the slightest effort, by mere growth it would seem, he passed on into the "Chamber of Maiden Thought," as he phrased it, and became absorbed as deeply in his reflections as previously in his impulses. At no time, indeed, was he wholly unthoughtful. The passages that have been given above are parenthetical, and should be read in connection with such as these, of the opposite tenor : —

" I must think that difficulties nerve the spirit of a man; they make our prime objects a refuge as well as a passion."

" I am becoming accustomed to the privations of the pleasures of sense. In the midst of the world, I live like a hermit. I have forgot how to lay plans for the enjoyment of any pleasure. I feel I can bear anything, — any misery, even imprisonment, — so long as I have neither wife nor child."

" Women must want imagination, and they may thank God for it; and so may we, that a delicate being can feel happy without any sense of crime."

" Scenery is fine, but human nature is finer; the sward is richer for the tread of a real nervous English foot; the eagle's nest is finer for the mountaineer having looked into it."

Many a remark, based like these immediately upon his own experience, shows that Keats had an insight into his own life and an outlook on the world inconsistent with the portrayal of him as merely impassioned with sensuous beauty.

So far, in fact, was Keats from being either lapped in Lydian airs or fed on food of sweetest melancholy that he was sometimes a disagreeably unhappy person, if his brother George's description of him be entirely true, since his moodiness was vented in complaints, irritable jealousies, and like ways. However exceptional such occasions were in the intercourse of the brothers, this exposure, taken together with some of the upbraidings in the letters to Fanny Brawne, is very significant. Keats himself refers to the strain of morbidity in him, and, although from time to time he felt the strong awakening of the philanthropic instinct, frequently expresses his distaste for society, his misanthropy, his indifference to the public, his wish to live withdrawn, free from human relations, engaged in poetizing for his own sake. Toward women especially he had a

bitter tongue, before he fell in love with
Fanny Brawne.

"When I was a schoolboy, I thought a
fair woman a pure goddess; my mind was a
soft nest in which some one of them slept,
though she knew it not. . . . When I am
among women, I have evil thoughts, malice,
spleen; I cannot speak or be silent; I am
full of suspicions, and therefore listen to
nothing; I am in a hurry to be gone. You
must be charitable, and put all this perver-
sity to my being disappointed since my boyhood. Yet with such feelings I am happier
alone, among crowds of men, by myself, or
with a friend or two."

He ascribes this peculiarity to his love for
his brothers, "passing the love of women:"

"I have been ill-tempered with them, I
have vexed them, — but the thought of them
has always stifled the impression that any
woman might otherwise have made on me."

He saw but little to choose, in his satirical
moods, between men and hawks: —

"The hawk wants a mate; so does the
Man. Look at them both; they set about it
and procure one in the same manner; they
want both a nest, and they set about one
in the same manner. The noble animal

man, for his amusement, smokes a pipe; the hawk balances about the clouds: that is the only difference of their leisures."

Experience did not teach him more charity, though it made him more discriminating:—

"The more I know of men the more I know how to value entire liberality in any of them. Thank God, there are a great many who will sacrifice their worldly interest for a friend. I wish there were more who would sacrifice their passions. The worst of men are those whose self-interests are their passions; the next, those whose passions are their self-interest. Upon the whole, I dislike mankind. Whatever people on the other side of the question may advance, they cannot deny that they are always surprised at hearing of a good action and never of a bad one."

This temper toward man in the abstract is the general feeling of which his mood toward the public is a special instance. He simply disregarded men who stood in no intimate relation to him, whether he met them in society or wrote verses for them to read. He was not, if his word be literally taken, sensitive to criticism or ambitious of popularity: he neglected the one because he put faith in his own judgment, and he despised the other because it was to be got at a vulgar cost. His depreciation of the life of men, as he saw it, arose partly from a consciousness of power, partly from a sense of the distance between his thoughts and hopes and those of his fellows. The aloofness of genius he had in full measure. That curiously complex emotion, into which so many instincts and perceptions enter that it is scarcely analyzable at all, and is forced to go under the name of pride, was often dominant in his moods when others than his friends were before his attention. In short, Keats was as incompatible with his surroundings as ever any young poet left to the oblivion of his own society ; and he was as indignant at stupidity, as tired of insignificance, as thoroughly world-weary, as a solitary enthusiast for the ideal could well be. In his last letter to George he sums the whole matter up more fully than at first but to the same purport : —

" 'T is best to remain aloof from people, and like their good parts without being eternally troubled with the dull process of their every-day lives. When once a person has smoked the vapidness of the routine of society, he must either have self-interest or the love of some sort of distinction to keep him in good humor with it. All I can say is that, standing at Charing Cross and looking east, west, north, and south, I can see nothing but dullness. I hope while I am young to live retired in tho country. When I grow in years and have a right to be idle, I shall enjoy cities more."

In this opinion he did retire to one place or another, — the Isle of Wight, or Winchester, or Teignmouth, and there isolating himself dreamed out his poems. He lived in a sort of ecstasy during no small portion of these solitary hours, when he could call the roaring of the wind his wife, the stars through the window panes his children, and rest contented in the abstract idea of beauty in all things. This absorption in the idea of beauty which determined the formulation of his creed in the oft-quoted lines, —

> " Beauty is truth, truth beauty, — that is all
> Ye know on earth, and all ye need to know ; "

which also led him into that much misunderstood exclamation, " O for a life of sensations rather than of thoughts ; " this intoxication, as it were, with the loveliness of earth, was in his belief a true Pythian inspiration, the medium of the divine revelation. The world takes such expressions as extravaganzas, or as mystical philosophy; but to Keats they were as commonplace as the proverbs of the hearth; he meant them as entirely lucid expressions of plain sense. This point in the criticism of Keats has been too little insisted on and brought to notice. He put his faith in the suggestions of the spirit; he relied on the intimations of what is veiled from full sight; he had little patience with minds that cannot be content with half-knowledge, or refuse to credit convictions because they cannot be expressed in detail, with logical support, and felt with the hand of sense all round, if one may employ the phrase; in other words, he believed in the imagination as a truth-finding faculty, not less valid because it presents truth in a wholly different way from the purely logical intellect. This was the deepest and most rooted persuasion of his mind from the time when he first comes under our observation. To bring together a few expressions of it is the only right way of setting forth his creed in this matter. The following extracts are from various parts of his letters, from the earliest to the later ones: —

"At once it struck me what quality went to form a man of achievement, especially in literature, and which Shakespeare possessed so enormously — I mean *negative capability*, that is, when a man is capable of being in uncertainties, mysteries, doubts, without any irritable reaching after fact and reason. Coleridge, for instance, would let go by a fine isolated verisimilitude caught from the penetralium of Mystery, from being incapable of remaining content with half-knowledge. This pursued through volumes would perhaps take us no further than this, that with a great poet the sense of Beauty overcomes every other consideration, or rather obliterates all consideration."

"Many a man can travel to the very bourne of heaven, and yet want confidence to put down his half-seeing."

"I never feel quite certain of any truth but from a clear perception of its beauty, and I find myself very young-minded, even in that perceptive power."

"The whole thing must, I think, have appeared to you, who are a consecutive man, as a thing almost of mere words. But I assure you that, when I wrote it, it was a regular stepping of the imagination toward a truth."

" What the imagination seizes as beauty
must be truth, whether it existed before or
not. . . . The imagination may be compared
to Adam's dream — he awoke and found it
truth.   I am more zealous in this affair because I have never yet been able to perceive
how anything can be known for truth by
consecutive reasoning, and yet [so] it must
be. . . . However it may be, O for a life of
sensations rather than of thoughts !   It is a
' vision in the form of youth,' a shadow of
reality to come."

A shadow of reality to come !   What a
light that sentence throws on the aspiration for sensations rather than thoughts, for
beauty rather than logic, for the sight rather
than the inference, for the direct rather than
the mediate perception of the divine !   So,
at least, it is plain, Keats understood himself ; and whether one counts his faith a
vague self-deception, meaningless except to
a mystic, or has found the most precious
truth borne in upon his heart only by this
selfsame way, the recognition of the. poet's
philosophy not merely lifts Keats out of and
above the sphere of the purely sensuous, but
reveals at once the spiritual substance which
underlies his poetry, and which gives it vi-

tality for all time. To other men beauty has been a passion, but to him it was a faith; it was the substance of things hoped for, the evidence of things unseen, — *a shadow of the reality to come.* It was not, as with other poets, in the beauty of nature, the beauty of virtue, the beauty of a woman's face, singly that he found his way to the supra-sensible; he says in his most solemn words, " I have loved the principle of beauty *in all things.*" Dying he said it proudly, as one who had kept the faith that was given him; and since he chose that declaration as the summary of his accomplishment, it needs to be borne in mind, with all its large and many-sided meaning, by those who would pluck out the heart of his mystery.

But although to Keats the worship of beauty in all things was the essence of his life, and the delight that sprang from it the essence of his joy, he did not find in these the whole of life. At first he had been satisfied if the melancholy fit fell on him, " sudden from heaven, like a weeping cloud," — eager to let the passion have its way with him, until it wreaked itself upon expression; but he felt this overmastering of his own will an injury, not merely exhausting but wasteful.

"Some think I have lost that poetic ardor and fire 't is said I once had ; — the fact is, perhaps I have ; but, instead of that, I hope I shall substitute a more thoughtful and quiet power. I am more frequently, now, contented to read and think, but now and then haunted with ambitious thoughts, . . . scarcely content to write the best verses for the fever they leave behind. I want to compose without this fever. I hope I one day shall."

Similarly, he wishes to know more, and is determined to "get learning, get understanding," if only that he may keep his balance in the "high sensations" that draw him into their whirl.

" Although I take poetry to be the chief, there is something else wanting to one who passes his time among books and thoughts on books. . . . I find earlier days are gone by — I find I can have no enjoyment in the world but continual drinking of knowledge. I find there is no worthy pursuit but the idea of doing some good to the world. . . . There is but one way for me. The road lies through application, study, and thought. I will pursue it ; and, for that end, purpose retiring for some years."

The years that should have perfected his powers were denied to him; his account was made up. In these broken plans, however; in this constant expansion of his view and faithful laying of his experience to heart; in the wisdom of his interpretation of what came within his scope; in a word, in his teachableness as well as in his steadier enthusiasm, his uncloyed sensibility, his finer spirituality, as the promise of Keats seems brighter, so his worth seems greater. These letters show that more had passed into his character than was ever reproduced in his poems. We come back to Lord Houghton's decision. Fine as the work of Keats is, his genius was, nevertheless,

> " The bloom, whose petals, nipt before they blew,
>   Died on the promise of the fruit."

It has been suggested in some quarters that, notwithstanding his early death, he would probably have done no better work, if indeed he even maintained himself at the height he had reached. In support of this it is urged that Wordsworth's best poetry was written in youth, and that Coleridge's powers were employed on really excellent verse only for two years. These letters make it folly to entertain such a belief;

they (and the works too) exhibit not only
an increase of intellectual, but also of artistic power. No criticism of his poetry is intended here ; but, in connection with this
point, it may be remarked that his principal defect is in style, as is shown by the
necessity he continually felt of studying literary models, which nevertheless affected his
productions hardly at all, except in linguis-
tic handling, — in the choice and flow of
words, after Spenser, the structure of sentences, after Milton, and later (in Lamia),
after Dryden, and in a movement and kind
of verbal *esprit*, after Ariosto. This restless
change from one master to another, as well
as some few critical remarks, indicates a
power to form a distinctive style of his own.
Again, the marked pictorial character of his
poetry — the quality it has to impress one
like a cartoon or a bas-relief (" the brede
of marble men and maidens "), the grace of
form and attitude in the figures of his poetic
vision — was clearly recognized by him to
be in excess in his compositions. Originally,
this was due, in a high degree, to the acci-
dent of his friendship with Haydon ; the
portfolios of the masters helped his imagination in definiteness, in refinement, and es-

pecially in power of g "ping. As the mind
became more to him, and the eye less, he
was dissatisfied with this trait of his works.
He condemned even the most perfect composition of this kind in English: "I wish
to diffuse the coloring of St. Agnes' Eve
throughout a poem in which character and
sentiment would be the figures to such drapery." One who could speak of such a poem
as "drapery" was far from the conclusion
of his artistic education. Lastly, he was
from the beginning ambitious of writing
dramas. Otho and King Stephen are by no
means unmistakable prophecies of success,
had he continued in this hope. The effort,
however, proves an interest in humanity of
a different order from that shown in the
mythological or lyrical pieces, and makes
evident how far the naturalism of his pub-
lished poetry was from expressing the fullness of his mind. These three things — the
incipiency of his style, the acknowledged in-
sufficiency of picturesque art in creating the
best poetry, and the ardent desire to deal
with human life directly, and on the large
scale, in the drama — are enough to convince
us that Keats was truly a Chatterton, only
less unfortunate, — " born for the future, to

the future lost ; " one who, though he wears, Adonis-like, the immortal youth that lies in the gift of early death, would have been even dearer to the world, had his name lost in pathos and gained in honor, as it assuredly would have done if his grass-grown grave wore the wheaten garland of England instead of the Roman daisies.

AUBREY DE VERE ON POETRY.

IT is rare good fortune to find criticism in which the ideas are more excellent than the manner, and the spirit finer than the ideas; in which it is not the keener sympathy of the poet that speaks, or the sure sense of the trained artist for expression, or any single faculty, but the whole nature of the man; in which the judgment rendered does not proceed from any particular part of his mind — the scholarly or moral or æsthetic element by itself — but is felt to be grounded upon his total convictions. Aubrey de Vere's essays, therefore, are worth more than ordinary attention. He writes principally of Spenser and Wordsworth, and also of Milton, Shelley, and Keats. He considers mainly the doctrine of this poetry. He values it chiefly for its highest office as a teacher of moral wisdom, and a quickener of the spiritual part of our nature. He justly decides that its real subject is man's life; this is the centre of interest in all great thought, and the rest is but ornament and episode. He is a Christian idealist, and he refuses to regard poetry except in the light of those great ideas which belong to the spirit, and, being nobly and beautifully interpreted, are the substance of the poets who live by their wisdom as well as by charm. The ethical, the philosophical element in a large sense, is to him the engrossing thing; and criticism of this sort, so incited and so aimed, has a reality that does not fall far short of the worth of direct reflection upon the things of the mind, though it deals with them through the medium of literature instead of in life itself.

With Spenser, naturally, he has many affinities. The mediævalism, the sentiment of chivalry, the allegorizing spirit, and not less the Puritan elevation of the first of the Elizabethan poets, exercise a special fascination over a Catholic mind for whom the Ages of Faith, as he likes to call them, have in a peculiar degree the ideality that clothes the past. One no longer looks for original criticism of the father of English verse, who, more than Chaucer, may claim the paternity of great poets in later days; but to remind us of his excellence has become, in the lapse of time and the decline of poetic taste, almost as desirable an office as it once was to unfold its secret. Spenser is a poet who requires no common critic to speak justly of him. His position was a unique one, and by some infelicity of his stars he failed to rise to the greatness which seems to have been possible to him. Aubrey de Vere remarks that the great romantic poem of the Middle Ages, one that should sum them up on the human as Dante did upon the divine side, was never written ; and, looking back, it appears to us that Spenser was the choice spirit that missed this destiny. His pure poetic quality, that sensibility to beauty and delight in it as in his element, was perfect to such a degree that Milton and Keats, who possessed it in something of the same measure, seem almost to have derived it from him, whose poems nourished it in them. The sweetness and noble ease of his expression reveal the presence of a marvelous literary faculty. His responsiveness to the historical and legendary elements in the past, his power of abstracting and idealizing them for poetic use, and his profound interest in human life, were great endowments, and he possessed in a high degree and a pure form that moral reason which is the attribute of genius. But by defects as striking as this gift he made his poem less than we fondly think it might have been. The Elizabethan prolixity, the obscure perception of the nature of form in literary work, the artificiality incident to the allegorizing temperament, account for much of what he lost; but, for all that, his poems are marvels of the creative intellect, and it is this intellect that Aubrey de Vere dwells on. Any one can point out Spenser's loveliness, but the great spirit that brooded over his verse is not so easily realized. His aim was " to strengthen man by his own mind," and it is this effort which the critic analyzes, and by so doing tries to show how well he deserved the epithet "grave " as well as " gentle Spenser."

His work, with its intricate allegory, its machinery of faëryland and chivalry, its ideal landscape, is regarded as remote from life; but just as the creations of art, which also have this unreality, are yet the expression, oftentimes, of the most real human feeling and the most substantial thought of the mind, so the figures of his embroidered poem compose a procession of true life. They are conceived and used in accordance with a comprehensive doctrine of the nature of humanity, which Spenser undoubtedly meant to enforce through the medium of the imagination; this doctrine, in fact, is the stuff they are made of.

It is not an easy thing to resolve into its moral elements the creations of a poet who blends many strains of truth. His method is not the consecutive process of logical reflection and explication, but the simultaneous embodiment of what, however arrived at, he presents as intuitive, needing only to be seen, to be acknowledged. In the analysis, the distinctive poetic quality is too apt to be dissipated, and the poet is forgotten in the philosopher. Certain broad aspects may be easily made out. Chivalry, with its crowd of faëry knights, certainly rests, in Spenser's great work, upon the old conception of the Christian life as one militant against the enemies of the soul in the world; and quite as clearly he also represents this life as being, within the breast, ideal peace. Peace within and war without: these are two root-ideas out of which the poem flowers on its great double branches. He teaches specifically how to attain self-control, and how to meet attacks from without; or rather how

to seek those many forms of error which do
mischief in the world, and to overcome them
for the world's welfare. This is a bald statement, but it indicates well enough in what
way Spenser employed the knightly ideal of
succor on the one hand, and the Christian
ideal of moral perfection on the other, in order to make a poem which should instruct
as well as delight the world. He himself asserts that his aim was so lofty, and to a man
such as he was a lower aim, a merely artistic
purpose, would have been impossible. It is
fortunate that he was not less endowed with
the sense of loveliness than with a serious
mind ; for he thus illustrates not only the
possible union of the two principal aims of
poetry in all times, but also the truth that
to a man whose perception of beauty is most
perfect the beauty of holiness is the more
impressive and authoritative in its com-
mands. Aubrey de Vere devotes himself
especially to the declaration and the proof
that Spenser's poetic character was essentially that of a man deeply interested in
human life, and he tries to prevent the
poet's severely ideal, and sometimes fantastic, method from obscuring, as for many
minds it does, the real nature of that alle-

gory, so marvelous for invention, eloquence, and perpetual charm of style, which is seldom thought to be more than an intricate and lovely legend of the imagination. The critic is not blind to the great defects of the work, — and no poem of equal rank has more, — nor does he neglect the excellences that are obvious to the least thoughtful reader; but he succeeds in placing before us its intellectual and moral substance.

In doing this he reveals his own theory of poetry, and it is one that derives its philosophy from the great historic works of our literature, and is grounded on the practice of the English masters whose fame is secure. Its cardinal principle is that man is the only object of interest to man, all else being subordinate, and valuable only for its relations to this main theme; and more particularly this subject is the spiritual life, not the material manifestations of his energies in deeds apart from their meaning. The Italian masters of Spenser too often lost themselves in incident, in romance, in story for its own sake; they were destitute of that ethical spirit which insists on planting in the deeds their significance, and regarding this as an integral, and indeed the only immortal, part of the action. The laws of life, not the chances of individuals, were Spenser's subject, and in this he differs from Ariosto, and leaves his company. Spenser's genius was thus abstract and contemplative, and Platonic in the sense that he used images always with some reference to the general truths that transcend imagination, and are directly apprehended only intellectually. Allegory was therefore his necessary method. Spenser never succeeded in harmonizing the disparate elements of the material to which he fell heir by literary tradition; and besides the inconsistencies and incoherencies of the Renaissance culture, which never reached any unity in its own time, there were also special disturbances in his intellectual life because of the political and religious conflicts in England itself, from entanglement with which he was not free; and, moreover, he does not seem to have subdued the philosophical and poetic impulses of his own nature to any true accord. His poem, therefore, did not take on that perfection, that identity of purpose and execution, which would have placed it in the first rank, and he remains below the supreme poets of the world. The study of his work, as an illustration of the conditions and art of poetry, is most instructive. Its defects teach more than its excellence, but they do not disturb the theory which Aubrey de Vere sets forth; and he would be but a blind critic who should easily argue that Spenser succeeded when he obeyed the pure artistic impulse, and failed because of the interference of his graver genius with the poetical mind, his thought with his sensibility.

Aubrey de Vere's contemplative mind, his strong hold on the abstract rather than on the concrete, help him over the poetically dry places in Spenser, and serve him even better in the case of Wordsworth. This is choosing the better of two alternatives; for, if the landscape of Arcady is incomplete for him unless there is some " swan -flight of Platonic ideas " over it, such as he says is always in Spenser's sky, he has an appreciation for beauty as steadfastly as for the higher truths of life, and it is better to suffer with deficiencies in poetic art for the sake of the matter than to be content with art alone.

The great difference between Wordsworth and Spenser is, that Spenser was concerned with the moral virtues and man's acquirement of them, while Wordsworth was more narrowly limited to the influence of nature in forming the soul. Both looked to the same end, — spiritual life; but Wordsworth had a different starting-point. His mind was more individual, and he assumed that his own history was typical; he was less rich in the stores of antiquity, and he had less sensibility to beauty in its ideal forms; but he knew the place that nature held in his own development, and he became specifically the poet of nature, not only as beauty visible to the eye, but also, and mainly, as an invisible influence in the lives of men. Much of his verse was a pastoral form of philosophy; meditation counted for more than beauty in it; but the scene was the English country, and the characters were rustics. There was, too, something of imaginative untruth in it, no doubt, similar to that inherent in all pastoral poetry. These common men, however, were not individuals, but stood for man, and Wordsworth, in delineating their histories, was writing a parable as well as a story. In other portions of his verse he used a more abstract method. As a moralist he was much given to maxims; and in all that concerns the social and political life of man, as well as his personal relations to

virtue, Wordsworth was, as the critic affirms
with much emphasis, filled with a certain
ardor, which may be called passion if one
likes. The lack of passion in the ordinary
sense — and it cannot be made out that
Wordsworth possessed this quality — only
renders more plain the moral endowment of
the poet, his absorbing interest in the manly
virtues, and the supreme value which he
placed on the spiritual life and its ideal relations. He considered these relations most directly as existing toward nature, and having
their operation in the emotion which nature
excites. He did not altogether escape from
the pantheism incident to such a constant
preoccupation of the mind with the works
and course of nature, and consequently he is
less distinctively Christian than Spenser;
but Aubrey de Vere easily makes it out that
Wordsworth's philosophy, much as it differed
from Spenser's, is concerned with the same
topics of moral and spiritual life, and is the
substance of his poetry.

It is not surprising that a writer of Aubrey de Vere's temperament is annoyed by
the charge that Wordsworth is destitute of
" passion." He has much to say on this
point. Wordsworth himself gave as the rea-

son why he did not write love-poems the fear that they would be too passionate. Aubrey de Vere makes what defense he can by pointing out the half-dozen idealizations of woman in the shorter lyrics; but his real apology consists in the counter-assertion that Wordsworth is especially distinguished for " passion." He uses the word, however, with a difference, and means by it the poetic glow, the exaltation of feeling, the lyrical possession, which attends the moment of creation and passes into the verse. Of this sort of passion every form of poetry is as capable as is the amorous: the *sæva indignatio* of satire would come under this head as properly as the moral enthusiasm or the patriotic fervor shown in the Ode to Duty or the Sonnets. Wordsworth truly possessed this capability, and it gives to his poems their masculine strength. Whether equal success is to be credited to the critic's glosses upon the more commonplace subjects of Wordsworth's muse, is doubtful; it seems rather that he makes the mistake which Coleridge attributed to Wordsworth himself, of giving a value to the idea which it has in his own mind, but which it does not have in the bare words addressed to the reader. When the idea and the expression are not identical, every poet suffers from this cause; in his mind the idea, coming first, dignifies the words, but to the reader the words coming first, too often mutilate the idea. It is a good result of Aubrey de Vere's Wordsworthianism that it gives him courage to force into the front of his essay the Orphic Odes, which are among the least known of the poet's work, and contain some of the noblest of his lines.

To Milton he seems somewhat unjust. The earlier poems receive his warm appreciation, but of the later ones he is hardly so tolerant, and nowhere does he give him his due. This is the passage: —

"It is not, however, its deficient popularity so much as its subject and its form which proves that Milton's great work is not a national poem, high as it ranks among our national triumphs. Some will affirm that he illustrated in that work his age if not his country. His age, however, gave him an impulse rather than materials. Puritanism became transmuted, as it passed through his capacious and ardent mind, into a faith Hebraic in its austere spirit — a faith that sympathized indeed with the Iconoclastic zeal

which distinguished the anti-Catholic and
anti-patristic theology of the age, but held
little consort with any of the complex defini-
tions at that time insisted on as the symbols
of Protestant orthodoxy. Had the Puritan
spirit been as genuine a thing as the spirit
of liberty which accompanied it; had it been
such as their reverence for Milton makes
many suppose it to have been, the mood
would not so soon have yielded to the licen-
tiousness that followed the Restoration. . . .
To him the classic model supplied, not the
adornment of his poem, but its structure
and form. The soul that wielded that mould
was, if not exactly the spirit of Christianity,
at least a religious spirit — profound, zealous, and self-reverent — as analogous, perhaps, in its temper to the warlike religion
of the Eastern Prophet as to the traditional
faith of the Second Dispensation. Such was
the mighty fabric which, aloof and in his
native land an exile, Milton raised; not perfect, not homogeneous, not in any sense a
national work, but the greatest of all those
works which prove that a noble poem may
be produced with little aid from local sympathies, and none from national traditions."

Some expressions in this passage, and

many others scattered through these volumes, indicate where the current of sympathy was broken by default of which the critic understands Milton imperfectly. Ideal he was, but there is no poet who is more bone and flesh of the English nation in the substance of his genius, or in whom it developed a spirituality more noble; nor are his defects, in his conception of womanhood for example, such as cannot be easily paralleled from the other poets of highest genius in the line from Spenser. But, on the other hand, the critic is more than just to Keats, and towards Shelley he exhibits a respect, a penetration of the elements of his thoughtful temperament, and a comprehension of the remarkable and intimate changes of his incessant growth, that are almost unexampled in authors writing from Aubrey de Vere's standpoint. In writing of the others he has opportunity for still further illustration of the theory of poetry he holds, and he shows that these later poets have their best success the closer they keep to the subject of man, and the more they treat it with a pure, spiritual method; while on the other hand, they are defective in proportion as they fail in this.

It would be impossible for a critic with

such standards as these to pass in review the work of the moderns, and not to notice the general decline in the moral weight and the spirituality of late poetic literature. Materialism, both as respects the objects of man's pursuit and the character of his speculation in philosophy, has been so important and growing a factor of the times, that, if there is any validity in this theory of poetry, it must follow that our poetic work has lost elevation, meaning, and utility. Religion itself, so far as the general thought of nineteenth-century civilization is concerned, has suffered a diminution of its authority, and consequently the spiritual life of man has filled a less prominent part in the eyes of these generations.

In connection with this, room should be made for some original remarks of the writer upon the Pagan element in our modern poetry. He is very well affected towards Platonism, and recognizes it historically as "the chief secondary cause of the diffusion of Christianity, doing for it more than the favor of Constantine could ever have done." He thus affirms for Greek religion and Greek philosophy "an element of greatness and truth." Our poets, in returning to its life and thought, seem to him to be making a return to the spiritual element which in the revolutionary ages has been obscured and too often lost. He speaks in this as a Catholic, but he is more Christian than Catholic, if it may be permitted to say so; and all religious writers admit and lament the inroad of skepticism and consequent materialism. The turn he gives to these facts is a striking one: —

"The arts of the Middle Ages soared above Paganism: the imaginative mind of modern times stands for the most part aloof from it; but it often stands aloof from Christianity also. Secularity is its prevailing character, while even in Paganism there is a spiritual element. We may not, without a risk of insincerity and presumption, indulge in either an exultation or a regret higher than corresponds with our low position. Can we with truth say that the portion of our modern literature which reverts to ancient mythology is less religious than the rest? Is it not, in the case of some authors, the only portion which has any relations, even through type or symbol, with religious ideas? Would Dante, would even Milton, have found more to sympathize with in the average of modern literature than in Homer or in Sophocles, in Wordsworth's Laodamia or Keats's Hymn to Pan? What proportion of our late poetry is Christian either in spirit or in subject — nay, in traditions and associations? Admirable as much of it is, it is not for its spiritual tendencies that it can be commended. Commonly it shares the material character of our age, and smells of the earth; at other times, recoiling from the sordid, it flies into the fantastic. . . . It is our life which is to be blamed; our poetry has been but the reflection of that life."

This is valuable, not only for its suggestion, but because it sums up and speaks out plainly the protest which is implicit in all this criticism. The æsthetic lover of beauty, the artist who is satisfied with feats of poetic craft, will not find anything to his liking in Aubrey de Vere's essays. They are presided over by a severe Platonism intellectually, by an exacting and all-including Christianity when the subject touches upon man's life, and they will prove somewhat difficult reading, perhaps, because the thought continually reverts to great ideas, to that doctrine of life which the author seeks for in the poets, and prizes as the substance of their works. But it is well, in poetic days like these, to be brought back to the more serious muses which inspired the great ideal works of our literature, and to converse with them under the guidance of such a spirit as fills these essays with a sense of the continual presence in great literature of the higher interests of man, his life on earth, and his spiritual relation to the universe. These essays contain the fruits of habitual familiarity with poetry, the convictions of a lifetime with regard to those things which are still important subjects of thought to thoughtful men; and there is, mingled with the style, the sweet persuasiveness of a refined and liberal nature, which is only too well aware that it must plead its cause, and pleads with strength and charm.

ILLUSTRATIONS OF IDEALISM.

I. THE PERGAMON MARBLES.

THE development of the Greek genius in sculpture, after it had passed its first maturity in Phidias and his immediate successors, presented the same characteristic signs shown in the history of other modes of artistic expression in other nations. A reasoned conception of the ends and means, a trained appreciation of form, a complete mastery of technique, were inherited by the sculptors of Pergamon. The purpose being defined and the tools perfected, no originality was allowed them except in style; and consequently their work, like the last dramas of Shakespeare, or the creations of Browning or Carlyle, exhibits an excess of subject, an effort to put the utmost of muscular action, of narrative import, of allegorized truth, into their marbles. And yet, in connection with this intensity, as it is called, it cannot fail to be observed that their sculpture (herein touched with the decadence) breathes the self-glorifying spirit of triumphant skill, rather than the overmastering idealism of the earlier patriotic and religious motives. In their pictorial composition and landscape backgrounds, also, one is tempted to discern the harmful influence of that so vaguely known school of painting that flourished in the preceding period, and to piece out by conjecture our fragmentary conceptions of its manner. It is complained that modern sculpture is too pictorial; almost as soon as the art was recovered in Italy it fell into the same error, particularly in relief work; but in Greece the profuse use of color on the marble, as ground and also for direct decoration, together with the employment of metals and jewels as additional adornment, must have brought the two arts so closely together that the transference of modes of treatment was inevitable. The striking thing is that painting, then as now, seems by its greater compass to overpower its more hampered rival.

Besides this tendency to overtax the power of expression by the weight of subject, and this pride in mere technique in close association with a humiliating imitation of a different art, these Pergamon sculptures display other marks of being essentially quite modern. Their realism is especially noticeable. The Greeks of the elder time, it must be acknowledged, were remarkably fortunate in that their realistic spirit fell in with an actual existence which itself appealed to the imagination in many ways. In the Athenian prime the life that taught Sophocles and Agathon was heroic or idyllic, and needed hardly a touch to exalt its elements into the most imaginative idealism. When Plato could not write a dialogue without making a drama, nor Aristophanes compose a comedy without breaking into the sweetest lyric song, nor Phidias chisel a flying fold except for eternity, a presence was upon the earth and a spirit in men that made realism not less trustworthy as a guide to sculptors than is the "Look into thy heart and write" as a maxim for poets like Sidney. But when the barbarians broke in from the north upon Asia Minor, and the luxury of oriental manners and the fantasies of oriental mind stole upon the old order and changed it, to study the real was not necessarily to achieve the beautiful. The barbarians chiseled by the Pergamon sculptors are very different

from those that once adorned the Parthenon : they are fierce, ugly, portrait-like, stud-
ied from the life. The giants, too, by the
same artists are not even altogether human,
as in the older reliefs, but many are mon-
strous : conglomerates of snaky folds and
Titanic limbs and ox necks, finny wings,
pointed ears, horns, and such Egyptian and
Assyrian confusions. For this debasement
of the type, few will consider the wonderful
finish, the minute and successful imitation
of fur, scale, and stuff, a compensation. So,
too, the representation of mortal agony is,
in these works, carried to an extreme of
truthfulness that is upon the verge of the
revolting. This new bent of realism which,
ceasing to select from the beautiful in life,
now takes these three directions, — toward
the portraiture of types not noble, toward
the close copying of accessories not important, and toward the reproduction of shocking aspects of existence, — this essential difference between the art of Athens and of
Pergamon, it would be but too easy to parallel in more than one province of our own
intellectual life. These remarks, although
they were not meant to point such a moral,
incidentally illustrate how misleading is the

the word "ancient" when applied to the Greeks. Wherever approached, they are as level to our own times in thought and deed as any of the so-called moderns; and though their language, in its former dialect, is dead, its golden words always fall upon our ears as if from the lips of some wiser contemporary. In looking on these recovered marble fragments, just as in reading the Antigone or Alcestis, the centuries seem meaningless.

II. A GREEK TRAIT NOTICED BY DR. WALD-STEIN.

One distinction between the Greeks and ourselves may be expressed by saying that our culture as a people rests upon literature, on the printed word, while that of the Greeks based itself rather upon observation, on the thing seen. The divergence of intellectual mood thus induced between ancient and modern is profound, and affects the whole higher life. In reflecting upon this classical trait, however, something is to be guarded against. It is well known that the illiterate, generally speaking, think in images, and that this power or habit of visualization, sometimes thought to be characteristic of the poet, be it observed, usually falls into disuse in proportion to the increase and continuity of exclusively literary culture in the individual, until the point is reached at which a man thinks without having a single image definitely projected upon the mind's eye; his mental processes are, in fact, as colorless and formless as algebraic calculations. Mr. Galton's experiments in this matter are still fresh in our memories. Now it is not to be inferred that this was always the case, nor indeed that the intellect of highest development may not in the past, at least, have habitually thought in images, as the unlettered do to-day; and in Greece it appears that the picture language of the mind, as one may call it, held a place more important than with us, and perhaps equivalent to our own idea language. The Greek, as every one knows, peopled the earth with presiding geniuses, of more or less exalted rank, from Oread and Naiad, to the great Zeus of Olympus. These forms we call imaginary, and to our thought they are always tenuous; the point to be remembered is that, when the Greek spoke of Athene, an image came before his mind, and one not hypothetical and consciously symbolical, like Liberty with her cap, but definite, real, and awful, like the statue on the pediment or in the temple. The Greek mind leaned on these images as our mind does on the alphabet in all mental life; hence the poetry and the art of the age had a certain ease and naturalness, an intimacy with things seen by the eye, not equaled in the work of later times, except possibly in Italy. Dr. Waldstein points out that the most striking expression of this plastic necessity, inherent in Greek thinking, is the doctrine of Platonic ideas. To the moderns, however tolerant they may be, there seems always a childishness, a grotesque quality, the more marked because of Plato's splendid and rich endowment, in the continual insistence in his philosophy on the "ideas" of the table and the flute,—the table without any definite number of legs, the flute without any particular quality of sound; and the case is not much helped, even if one perceives, as Schopenhauer shows, that the doctrine is essentially accurate in truth, and wholly intelligible, since it is merely the modern statement of the subjectivity of time and space put conversely. Notwithstanding these admissions, our minds still find the Platonic ideas awkward to deal with. But that Plato, at the end of his ab-

strusest speculations, and at the threshold of
one of the greatest generalizations of the human intellect, fell back upon the image-form-
ing faculty, and insisted on particularizing
the universal by means of a mystery or fiction of thought, is a crowning proof of the
pervasiveness and inner mastery of the plastic spirit in the culture of his civilization.

This trait of the Greeks has been dwelt
on, in the present instance, less for itself
than for its bearing on the idealism of the
art of Phidias, of which the marbles of the
Parthenon are the great examples. Of
course Dr. Waldstein, who knows the value
of this supreme achievement of the idealistic
temperament in man, is himself an idealist,
and when he has occasion to analyze the
monuments treats at more or less length of
the theory of idealism. He distinguishes at
once two kinds of physical representation,
the portrait and the type, and affirms an
analogous difference in representations of
the spirit that animates the stone, — the
man as he is, and the man as he ought to be.
He observes, too, that the Greeks were fortunately supplied with subjects of sculpture in
which both the physical and spiritual perfection of man were proper elements, and, in-

deed, requisite ; namely, the heroes and the gods. The higher life was the theme of their art in its greatest excellence, not as a possible but as an actual existence. This of itself was a valuable help to them, for centres of imagination were thus determined for them and given a certain external validity ; whereas among the moderns art is felt to be in its essence a mode of subjective creation, having no reality except in thought. The resulting sense of uncertainty, the weakened faith in such emanations of man's brain, almost inevitable for the contemporary poet or artist, is one cause of the recoil of our imagination from the ideal, and of the attraction of realism for our writers, and perhaps of our content with a literature and art that will have fact for its province. "Let us have facts," is the cry ; "of truth — that is, the relation of facts — who can be certain? Let us represent men as they are ; of men as they ought to be who has any observation?" And even within these limits of the new school it is said, furthermore, that attention is to be paid to the individual ; not to man as he is, but to this man, taken at random, as he is. The type is too general to be depicted, too far removed from actual seeing, too much an abstraction of the mind. It is plain that at the root of the difficulty felt by the realists who theorize in this way lies the conviction that the further the literary or any other representative art gets from the special fact, trait, or passion in its particular manifestation, the more vague, doubtful, pale, rubbed-out, — in a word, the more generalized, — it becomes, and hence loses sharpness, vigor, and illusiveness. But with the Greek the case was clearly quite otherwise. There was no loss of individualization in the type, whether of physical or of spiritual perfection. This Theseus or that Hermes is ideal; both are generalized from men, but they suffer no loss of vitality thereby. The idealism of Athens did not fade out in abstraction, but embodied the permanent elements of harmonious beauty in body and spirit, in forms " more real than living man." The habit of thinking in images, or with fixed associations of images, with general notions, was one reason for this success, undoubtedly; but before concluding that the literary and rationalizing culture of our day forbids us to hope for a similar blending of the type with individuality, let us remember that as with Phidias, so with Shakespeare: Hamlet is at once the type and the man. The poet born cannot turn aside, on this hand, into science, as the realists do; nor on that hand, into philosophy, as the allegorists do. To him that ideal art alone is possible in which the two are united in the expression of permanent and universal truth through selected facts.

Nevertheless, it may be urged, the Greeks passed rapidly from the idealistic to the realistic stage. And in connection with this one observes the happiness with which Dr. Waldstein identifies the elements of likeness between the Greeks and the moderns, just as he opposes their differences to each other. The most admirable example is an inquiry into the æsthetical qualities of the Hermes of Praxiteles, and in the course of it he delineates the characteristics of the age of Praxiteles, and parallels them with the traits of the time just subsequent to the French Revolution. In doing this he incidentally describes the common spirit in Shelley, Musset, and other representatives of an art, not of the noblest, but not of the worst either, of the interval after the great age, yet before the marked decadence. It may be said that the English never had an age of the Phidian kind; in European culture that is to be sought, if at all, in mediæval art. The Praxitelean age, however, was reproduced in essence in the first generation of our romantic period. A certain pathos, felt in view both of the world and of one's self, is perhaps its dominant quality, and with it go a sophistication, a self-consciousness, a reflectiveness, a slight yet not complete abstraction of the spirit from the object before it, illustrated by the expression of the head of Hermes in relation to the infant Dionysus on his arm. It is the mood of one whose spontaneous joy has been disturbed forever by thought. In such work one sees that the objective character of art, as it was in Phidias, is yielding to a new impulse; that the hold of the imagination on the divine and the eternal is slowly relaxing. At last, idealism went out in Greece, and, either in the shape of the portrait statues, or of such sculptures as those of Pergamon, realism came in to be the be-all and also the end-all of art.

Why was it, one asks, that the plastic nature of the Greeks did not preserve them, if the image-making faculty did in fact count so much in their development? How did they come to lose the ideal forms that sprang in the mind of Phidias when he thought of beauty and virtue? One cannot say that idealism failed, for its triumph in the Parthenon marbles marks the highest point ever reached by the human imagination in embodying its vision. It died out, and one says in explanation that the attention given to technique at last led to a disregard of the idea; or that the mere ability to reproduce details exactly was a temptation to apply art to deceptive imitation of the seen instead of to an illusive expression of the unseen; or that the age had lost the great ideas themselves, the perception of beauty and virtue, the belief in them and honor for them, and hence necessarily declined upon the things of this world, — that is, upon what is seen by the bodily eye rather than in the realm of thought and spiritual insight: and of these explanations perhaps one is as true as another, for they are all descriptions, from different standpoints, of what actually occurred. It is impossible, however, that in view of this history, and of the similar course in the development of mediæval painting, one should not ask him-

self whether the rise and defense of realism
among us mean that literature is to follow
in the same track, and die, as sculpture and
painting died, until a new age shall set the
wheel turning again; for if the history of
the arts teaches anything, it is that the ages
of idealism are the ages of power, and those
of realism the premonition and stiffening of
death.

III. MR. PATER ON IDEAL ÆSTHETICISM.

The heart of Mr. Pater's Marius lies
in his thought about the ideal, and it is in
the nature of all such thought to make a
peculiar demand upon the reader. Its wisdom is felt to be, as it were, sacerdotal, and
requires a conscious preparation of mind in
him who would know of it; its vision is
supernal, and disclosed only when some spiritual illumination has been sent before. So
runs a Platonic doctrine of election and
grace that has been held as rigorously in literature as in theology. This aristocracy of
idealism — its exclusiveness, its jealousy of
any intrusion of the common and worldly
within the company it keeps, its sense of a
preciousness, as of sacred things, within itself — is incorporate in every fibre of Mr.

Pater's work; and he makes the demand natural to it, not only implicitly by an unrelaxing use of such æsthetic and intellectual elements as appeal exclusively to the subtlest faculties of appreciation in their highest development, but explicitly also by the character of his hero. Marius, before he became an Epicurean, was moulded for his fate; his creator demanded an exceptional nature for the æsthetic ideal to react upon in a noble way, and so Marius was born in the upland farm among the fair mountains to the north of Pisa, and was possessed from boyhood of the devout seriousness, the mood of trustful waiting for the god's coming, which is exacted in all profound idealism. "*Favete linguis!* With the lad Marius there was a devout effort to complete this impressive outward silence by that inward tacitness of mind esteemed so important by religious Romans in the performance of their sacred functions." Marius was born one of the choice natures in whom the heavenly powers are well pleased; and emphasis must be given to this circumstance because it follows that the ideal life which he lived, deeply meditated though it is, is really an individual one. Marius is not typical, nor even illustrative in any broad way of the practice of æsthetic morals; and yet, since he is not national, nor local, nor historic, in his essential self, since he is more than an enlightened philosopher, and yet less than the enlightened Christian, since his personality approaches the elect souls of other ages, other sentiments and devotions, and yet is without any real contact with them, he is typical and illustrative perhaps of something that might be. This confusedness of impression springs from the fact that Mr. Pater, while he imagines in Italy, always thinks in London; he has modernized his hero, has Anglicized him, indeed, and nevertheless has not really taken him out of the second century. It was a bold thing to attempt. It was necessary for his purposes as an evangelist of ideal living, and perhaps within the range of moral teaching it is successful; but the way in which it was done is a main point of interest.

A Roman Epicurean, one suspects, was not unlike the proverbial Italianated Englishman. The native incompatibility between the distinctive Roman temperament and the light-hearted gayety of Greek sensuousness was similar to that between the

English and the Italian character in the later times; the perfection of Marius by means of a Greek ideal may run parallel with English culture under southern influences. There was, too, in Roman character a trait or two which brings it near to qualities that lie at the base of our own stock. Even in the Italian landscape there are Northern notes such as Mr. Pater mentions when Marius, in his walks to the coast, sees "the marsh with the dwarf roses and wild lavender, the abandoned boat, the ruined floodgates, the flock of wild birds." We are told, also, that "poetic souls in old Italy felt, hardly less strongly than the English, the pleasures of winter, of the hearth, with the very dead warm in its generous heat, keeping the young myrtles in flower, though the hail is beating hard without." This note of Marius's home-life and the love he had for it, with his particular regard for "Domiduca, the goddess who watches over one's safe coming home," and with the ideal of maternity that grew up in his memory of home, — this peculiarly English note is struck in the opening and is dominant at the end. Certain other characteristics ally this Etrurian boy with that nobler strain of

English blood, the Puritan strain as it was in Spenser. His instinctive seriousness, his scrupulosity of conscience, his inheritance of a certain sombreness from the stock that adorned the Etruscan funeral urns, his attachment to places and awe of some of them as sacred by the touch of a divine power, his sense of invisible enemies about his path, his rigorous self-discipline in preparation for certain hereditary sacred offices, a deadly earnestness at times, — as when he gazes so fixedly on the rigid corpse of his friend Flavian, — such are some of the traits that define his nature as essentially rather Northern than Southern, and provide a ground of special sympathy and understanding for us.

The second device by which Marius is modernized is by giving to him a power which, for one who runs as he reads, makes the character incredible. He is said to be affected sometimes in a way the opposite of the experience which many have who, on seeing a new place, seem to have been there before: Marius feels, in the most marked of his experiences, something that shall be, — he has always a prescience. Thus, in the cadence of Flavian's verses he hears the music of the Latin hymnology; in the sight

of his second friend, Cornelius, who displays
and puts on his armor of a Roman knight
in the dusty sunshine of the shuttered country - house, he foresees the Christian chivalry; in the faces and groups of the worship-
ers in Cecilia's house he discerns the serene
light and streaming joy of Giotto's and of
Dante's vision, and looks on the Madonna
and the Child that Raphael first painted.
In all this there seems an unreality; in
the Puritan Roman, the Cyrenaic Christian,
there is a sense almost of conscious artifice,
as if one were being befooled. And yet, as
for those Northern notes of landscape, cus-
tom, and character, scholarship can give
chapter and verse for them; and as for the
gift of prescience, — well, if it were impossible for Marius to have it, in a sufficient
measure at least, then the theory of ideal
living which he held to was at fault. And
this Marius, so constituted, his creator places
in an Italy over which the romantic desolation, which we know, was laying its charm of
dreamful decay, and in a Rome which, then
as now, was the huddled deposit of religions.

The intellectual conviction on which Marius conducted his life was simple and common enough, as must be the case with every

theory capable of being made a principle of living. The world is what we think it, and our part in existence is the fleeting moment of present consciousness. What shall be done with this moment? Economize it, said Marius, in dissent from the Stoic who said, "Contemn it." Economize it; make the most of the phenomena that arise in it, and see, so far as it depends on you, that these phenomena, both of sensation and idea, as they arise, are the most valuable possible to the moment; and so your experience — in other words, your life — will be the fullest and most refined. Above all, do not forget the main thing in this doctrine of economy, which is that the worth of experience depends, not on what it is at the moment in its detached and transitory phase, but on what it will prove in memory when it takes its place permanently and in relation to the whole of life. In such a scheme, receptivity, the most alert and varied powers of taking in impressions, is the one aim of cultivation. Here, too, much depended on the nature of Marius, this time on the side of his Southern endowment. An impressibility through sensation was his gift, his talent; and especially he was susceptible to what the eye observes:

he was one of those who are " made perfect by the love of visible beauty." This is the point of union of his life with the æsthetic ideal, and makes the story of it a pathway through scenes of loveliness not unlike, in a certain mild beauty, the frescoes on ancient walls. The narrative is pictorial, almost to the point of decoration, and moves always with an outlook on some fair sight. From the landscape of the villa where Marius was born — among those delightful Etrurian hills whence one looks to the marbled rifts of Carrara gleaming above olive and chestnut slopes, and gazes off through the purple sea-valley of Venus's Port, the noblest gateway of the descending sun — to the last throttling earthquake morning, a beautiful visible world is about us, and exercises its attractiveness both in nature and in humanity. The one end of Marius was to appropriate all this, to choose the best of sensation and its most nearly connected emotions, and to live in that. To do this involves a secondary talent, a gift of insight, a power to perceive relative values, which in reality means a faculty of moral discrimination; and just here one may easily fail to see whence Marius derived this.

Why was it, for example, that he, being so attached to sensation and the emotions that cling closest to it, rejected voluptuousness, with all its forms of beauty and joyfulness, as a thing essentially not beautiful nor joyful? What was it that kept him, the comrade of Flavian, who represents the pagan surrender to this life, pure, — so pure, indeed, that with his visionary sense he foresaw in chastity an ideal that was to be, and foreknew its coming beauty? A mere interpreter of character, an analyst, would say, that Marius obeyed in these choices his own nature, — that Puritan nature whose compulsion is always strong. He venerated his own soul and cherished its early instincts, and this was his salvation. But one might also give another explanation, which would seem more harmonious with the purpose of the author; one might say that what is moral is in its outward manifestation so clothed with beauty, visible beauty, that the man who looks for beauty only, the noblest, the ideal beauty, will find therewith the highest, the ideal good. It is essential to such a seeker that he shall look with his own eyes and be frank with himself; shall " look straight out " and acknowledge what he sees ; and this Marius does, thereby prefiguring in a way and practically making that " return to nature " which is the continually recurring necessity of all sincerity. If virtue does in fact wear this outward loveliness — and who would deny it ? — why may not the lover of beauty have truly seen the new and springing forms of goodness, recognized them, and taken their promise into his life ? In other words, was not that prescience of Marius merely a power of clear and honest seeing of the elements of beauty and ugliness there before him ?

That this is Mr. Pater's view of the matter is indicated most definitely by the contrast which he continually insists on between Marcus Aurelius and Marius, and which he brings out clearly in the attitude of these two toward the gladiatorial shows. In the amphitheatre Marius is conscious of the Emperor, the strenuous Stoic, as " eternally his inferior on the question of righteousness." The young Epicurean has a " decisive conscience on sight " which is indubitable, — that conscience which, in its condemnation of the great sin of an age, is the touchstone of the select few in it, and makes them on the side of the future and aware of its excellence to be, when " not to have been, by instinctive election, on the right side was to have failed in life." Aurelius, we are told, made the great mistake: *Vale, anima infelicissima!* is the last word of our author to him on the eve of the persecutions. And the reason is, that the Stoic was truly blind ; he had paltered with his senses until they lied to him, or spoke not at all. Marius saw the deformity of the evil, and, while rejecting it as something he might not see and live, chose the good by its beauty, and so selected in the midst of that Roman corruption the Christian elements in whose excellence the Church would triumph and be made fair.

There may be some surprise in perceiving in the evangel of æstheticism a morality of this height, a concentration of attention on the beauty of austerity, an exaltation of a noble Puritanism toward which the Cyrenaic ideal may lead. When this is understood, however, one finds it natural enough that the pervading tone of this history of an ideal life is really religious ; idealism, when it is living, cannot be otherwise than essentially religious. Nevertheless, it is a bold thing to put the question, as Mr. Pater implicitly does, whether an attention to the beautiful, to visible beauty, may not only be equivalent to moral discrimination and a safeguard of virtue, but also a mode of solving the ultimate religious questions of deity and man's relation to it. Marius does arrive at an intimation, perhaps a faith, that a protective divine companionship goes beside him, and at an emotion of gratitude to that unseen presence.

Two points only, in this wide branch of the speculation, can be dwelt on now. He says toward the end that he thinks he has failed in love; and here he touches on one weakness of his ideal, for it is only by love, as he perceives, that any reconciliation between the lover of beauty and the multitudinous pitiful pain which is so large a part of the objective universe can be obtained. The second weakness is perhaps greater. In his ideal there is both doubt and isolation; the subjective element in his knowledge, the exclusive reliance on his own impressions, the fact that in metaphysical belief the world is only his world, and in actual living the experience is individual, — all this holds in it a basis of ultimate incertitude. True and real for him it no doubt is, but is that, indeed, the necessary limit of knowledge and life ? In effect, too, his creed is Protestant ; independently of the necessary element of doubt in it, it has the isolating force inevitable to the believer who will accept only the results of his own examination by exercise of private judgment. This position is unsatisfactory ; and it seems to allow the rationality of that principle of authority by which an individual life obtains correction for its idiosyncrasies, cancels the personal error, and at the same time lets in upon itself the flood of the total experience of humanity summed up and defined in the whole body of the elect. Though stated here in terms of the Stoical philosophy, this is the Catholic conclusion. Or, if Marius does not quite assent to this, he does accept it in a half-hearted way as an hypothesis which is worth making since it reunites him to mankind. There is, it may be observed, a tendency toward Catholicism throughout the religious speculation. Another note of it, for example, is the attraction felt by Marius in the ritual of worship, as the perfection of that ceremonialism to which, in his boyish worship of the old gods, he was devoutly trained.

After all, at the end one still states the

promises of this æsthetic ideal, even when working on so unusual a nature as Marius's, interrogatively. Marius's life does not set it forth with convincing power. For one thing, it is not a vital life, but a painted one; and there is an inconsequence in the series of pictures, — they do not seem to follow one another by any iron necessity. It would be foolish to complain that a life avowedly only receptive and contemplative of the beautiful is inactive. Marius does nothing except at the end. Yet, within such limits, one never sees how beauty affected Marius or developed his soul, and though he is said to have got much from companionship, one sees love operant in him very seldom, and then it is a very silent and unexpressed love. He repeats his own epitaph, — *tristem neminem fecit,* — and it was true; but all his life seems negative, and continually one asks, How did he really live? and gets no answer. His whole life was a *meditatio mortis,* — that is all that is told us.

A sense of failure, or rather of incompleteness, oppresses one at the end of the narrative. Even granting that the success Marius is said to have achieved — one is never quite sure that he did — by that exquisite

appreciation of beauty and impassioned contemplation of its ideal forms, was, in fact,
his ; yet of what worth was it, — what did
it mean to either God or man ? The Northern idealist, the Puritan, cannot dispense
with some serviceableness as essential to
any high living. One should not push the
point too far, however. Independently of
all that has been said, any one who cares to
think on counsels of perfection for man's
life will find profound and original thought
about the ideal elements still at hand in
modern days for use, and many wise reflections, sown in this history. It is a rare
work, and not carelessly to be read. Some·
exquisiteness of taste, some delight in scholarship, some knowledge of what is best
worth knowing in the historic expressions of
man's aspiration, and, above all, that "inward tacitness of mind" the reader must
bring to its perusal. What of it? Have
we not the highest authority for casting our
pearls where Circe's herd cannot come?

IV. ITALIAN RENAISSANCE LITERATURE.

The traditional romance that hangs about
Italy has fostered a popular misapprehension
of nearly all things Italian. As the mother

of Christian art and the Catholic Church, the land is supposed to be religious ; as the long-enslaved and last-freed of the nations of Europe, the race is believed to be deficient in political sagacity. Yet it requires but little reflection, hardly more than a thought of the Reformation, to prevent surprise at the fact that the Italians were at heart the most irreligious of Christian peoples, and that the Church, viewed by them always as a secular institution, is a monument of their genius applied to practical affairs. Italian art, too, as an expression of national life, must be ascribed less to piety than to the native bent of mind, the inbred race disposition, which seeks to bring all spiritual things within the perception of the senses ; indeed, the course of development in Italian art lies principally in the gradual substitution of an æsthetic aim for a devout motive as the source of inspiration. No people is less dreamy, in the Northern sense ; the genius of the race is positive, definite, objective, practical, circumscribed in the tangible and visible facts of experience. Between Italian intellect and Italian feeling there seems to be no border-land. Ecstasy may fall from heaven and kindle masses of men into passion, as in the case of the Flagellanti, but it is a malady of emotion only; the madness passes, the mind remains untouched. In Dante's poem, as has been often pointed out, these race qualities are clearly apparent: the journey is mapped out as on a chart; the hours are duly reckoned; the world beyond is laid open to accurate observation; the dark places of his Comedy are not dark with the spirit's excess of light, but with mediæval metaphysics. In later authors, however different the subject, the temper of mind is the same. The grasp on reality is no less tenacious, the attention to detail no less careful; the incidents of the adventure, the look of the landscape, the physiognomy of the characters, no less plainly defined as phenomena ocularly seen.

In the poems of chivalry, whether romantic, heroic, or burlesque, which seem to possess the characteristics of later Italian literature in most variety, this realism is veiled by the apparent unreality of the fable. Arthur and Roland belong to the North; and to the Northern mind itself, although they have the substance of ideals, they are very remote. But the Arthur of Italian nobles, the Roland of the Italian people, are the

thinnest of shades; nor were they less in-
substantial to most of the poets of the golden
age than to us. The people gave the Caro-
lingian myth to them as the burden of their
stories; but, leaving Boiardo out of the account, they could not accept the conditions
of that imaginative world and believe in it;
nor could Boiardo, who had without doubt
a real enthusiasm for chivalry, believe with
Spenser's faith. Italy had no feudal past;
how could the citizen Pulci feel any living
sympathy with feudal ideals? The myth
was emptied of its moral contents; how
could Ariosto be earnest as Tennyson is?
In dealing with deeds of knight-errantry,
adventures in the lists and the forest, wizard
springs and invincible armor, all the poets
were conscious of something quixotic; to
Ariosto it was the main element. He could
not be serious; the mock gravity of irony
was the most he could compass. This sense
of unreality in the legend was not all that
led the last poets of the age especially to
play with their art. A more powerful reason was the hopelessness of society in their
age, deep as that which in earlier times fell
on their ancestors, who witnessed the barba-
rian incursions on Roman soil. Politically,

morally, and religiously, society was breaking up. What was there to be serious about? All that gives meaning to life was gone: the ties of family, country, and God were snapped. What better thing was there to do than to retire to the country, and let the world go " the primrose path " ? The striking thing in all this is, that the sense of the pleasure to be derived from the refinements of culture excluded from the minds of nearly all the most gifted Italians that gloom, which would have wrapped a Northern nation, at the sight of an anarchy which, if less terrible with blood than the French Revolution, was more appalling to the spirit. The Italians, however, went to their villas, to hear Bandello tell stories and Berni read verses. The City of the Plague, from which Boccaccio's garden party fled, is the permanent background of this golden age.

Life was something left behind, but art remained; and for the purposes of art, whose function was entertainment, the adventures of Orlando and his like were sufficiently serviceable. Such myths afforded opportunity for inexhaustible invention of incident, for the play of fancy, and the exhibition of the courtesies and humors of life;

and should there be a lapse into seriousness, there was room for satire on the clergy,
and for sentiments of the Reformation.
These tales, it is true, were products of culture separated from the realities of society,
and neglectful of them; but they were not,
as might have been anticipated, expressive
of individual rather than national temperament. They are prominently characterized
by the Italian love of incident, pictures, and
fun. The incidents are invented for their
own sake, not to develop character or exhibit
it in action; they are only adventures, hap-
penings, skillfully interwoven and rapidly
passed; but amid them the conduct of the
personages is true Italian, realistic. In presenting these incidents, and the scenes in
which they take place, the poets, as Lessing
complained, adopt pictorial methods: they
describe the ladies·piecemeal, the landscapes
leaf by leaf. Possibly, as has been suggested, the habitual sight of pictures ena-
bles the Italian to succeed where the German fails; to harmonize the colors on the
canvas and build up the fragments into a
proportioned statue, and thus obtain a single
mental impression. Whether this be so or
not, the pictorial quality is a tribute exacted

from literature by the ruling art, and illustrates the Italian proclivity to identify the mind's eye with the body's, to turn the things of the intellect into objects of sense. This realism, too, is shown as continuously in the frequent lapsing of Pulci's story, for example, into undisguised burlesque, low comedy, and broad fun; and more subtly in the prevailing irony of Ariosto. The poems thus constructed were an acceptable, usually a high, mode of amusement; they interested the fancy, delighted the senses, and stirred laughter. The Italians of the Renaissance asked no more.

In the prose tales, of which so many were written after the model of Boccaccio, the absorption of interest in simple incident is more plain, and the presence of contemporary manners more manifest. Various as they are, including every rank of life in their characters, and every phase of action in their events, they all bear a family resemblance. They are for the most part comedies of intrigue, arresting attention by romantic or piquant situations; usually immoral, not infrequently obscene. The crafty seducer is the text, the fool of a husband the comment; and when the gloss is read, afforded by the lives of the cardinals and the wit of the *capitoli*, no ground remains for doubting that they hold the mirror up to society as it then was. If they have any other than a humorous or romantic interest, it is the interest of the tragedy of physical horror, as in our English Titus Andronicus. Of course there are many stories to which this broad and rapid generalization would not apply, — tales wholly innocent, or harmless at least, full of movement, fancy, and action, graceful and charming with the art of story-telling at its Italian best; but, as a whole, they must be described as exhibiting a masque of sin. They are of the town in taste and temper; the corruption they set forth is not of the court or the curia only, but of the citizens; the laugh with which they conclude is an echo from the lips of the trades-people. Their principal value now is historic; they are the clear record of that social decay which condemned Italy to centuries of degradation. To ask why they did not generate the novel or suggest the drama is to state a literary puzzle; but the hundred considerations which have been put forth to explain the abortive issue of the miracle plays apply here also. It would seem as if the laws of spiritual development were unperceived; as if the knowledge of right and wrong as indestructible agencies to build or shatter character did not exist; as if the spirit had stiffened into that senseless stupor in which evil is no longer recognized for itself. It was left for the dramatists of the Globe Theatre to take these external incidents and show the meaning they had for humanity; to transfer the interest from the momentary and outer act, and centre it upon the living soul within. The Italians could not work the mines they owned; the pure gold of poetry that the novels held in amalgamation was to be the treasure of England. The works of the last years do not differ from the original of Boccaccio except for the worse; his successors never equaled their master; nor have their works obtained currency, like his, among men, as a part of the general literature of the cultivated world.

As the novelists make more prominent the realistic element of the narrative poems, the idyllic writers develop more plainly the pure poetic quality; in reading them one willingly assents to the enthusiasm which names their works the literature of the golden age. More than the epic or the novel, the idyl influenced the future. Arcadia is a well-known region in every great literature of Europe, and its atmosphere still hangs over the opera. The creator of this pastoral myth was the father of much beauty. Something was borrowed from the Garden of Eden, from the Virgilian fields, and from the Earthly Paradise; the religious, classical, and mediæval moods united in it; but essentially it was pure Italian, — Arcadia was an idealized Italy. The scene presented was the same country life that forms the background of all contemporary literature, but charmed, ennobled, and bathed in a softer than Italian air. There was little left in that age of ruin but delight in the natural beauty that was darkened by no shadow of humanity. The villa, the cultivated fields, the still, calm morning sky, were probably never more dear to the Italian heart than then, and it was this unsophisticated and keenly felt delight in nature that flowered in the idyl. To Northern nations Arcadia must always be a dream; to the Italians, then, at least, it was only the refinement of what was most real to them. It was because the idyl was so deeply rooted in a genuine emotion that it outlived the other modes of literature contemporary with it, and developed its final perfection only in the next age of the counter reformation in the art of Tasso and Guarini. But even in its earlier history the idyl shares with the best narrative poems that beauty of form which has conferred on both an immortality denied to the novel. The poets were all literary artists: they polished their verses with assiduous care; they expended many years in correction, elaboration, and adjustment; and they obtained that exquisite finish which, surface-like as it may seem, is adamant to the tooth of time. They achieved beauty, and won the delight that comes from its creation and contemplation; humor, too, they made their own, and gave it universal interest; they illustrated in practice the theory of art for art's sake; yet, after all, what is the judgment of posterity, we will not say on the men who were never suspected of being heroes, but on their works? They have left a literature, not of intellectual or moral weight, but of recreation; one that does not reveal, but amuses, — does not enlighten, inform, or guide life, but solaces and helps to while it away. This literature enriched the Northern minds by making them more sensitive to beauty, and by sharpening their perception of artistic refinements; it has left no other mark on civilization. The interest which the golden age excites in cultivated minds seldom loses its *dilettante* character; the really serious interest is in the Italy of Dante and Giotto, or in the genius of isolated men who stand apart, like Michel Angelo.

The Renaissance was a movement of civilization not less important than the Reformation or the Revolution, and to Italy, as its source, the debt of the world is great. But the Renaissance was not conveyed to Europe by the literature of its corruption; it was conveyed in far different ways.

REMARKS ON SHELLEY.

I. HIS CAREER.

THE natural charm by which Shelley fas-
cinated his familiar friends lives after him,
and has gathered about him for his defense
a group of men whose affection for him
seems no whit lessened because they never
knew him face to face. The one common
characteristic prominent in all who have
written of him with sympathy, however mea-
gre or valuable their individual contributions
of praise, criticism, or information, is this
sentiment of direct, intimate, intense personal loyalty which he has inspired in them
to a degree rare, if not unparalleled, in literary annals. Under the impulse of this
strong love, they have championed his cause,
until his fame, overshadowed in his own
generation by the vigorous worldliness of
Byron, and slightly esteemed by nearly all
of his craft, has grown world-wide. With
the enthusiasts, however, who have aided in
bringing about this result, admiration for

Shelley's work is a secondary thing; its virtue is blended with and transfused into the nature of Shelley himself, who is the centre of their worship. To reveal the fineness and lustre of his character, his essential worth throughout that romantic and darkened career of thirty years, is their chief pleasure, and in this, too, they have now won some success, and have partially reversed the popular estimate of the poet as merely an immoral atheist; yet, although some amends have been made for harsh contemporary criticism, Shelley's name is still for orthodoxy a shibboleth of pious terror and of insult to God. It is still too early to decide whether the modification of the harsh criticism once almost universally bestowed upon Shelley will go on permanently, or whether it is not in some measure due to peculiar results of culture in our own time. Without attempting to prejudge this question, especially in regard to poetic fame, there seems to be, as the cause passes out of the hands of those who knew Shelley personally into the guardianship of the new generation, a tendency toward greater unity of judgment in regard to the larger phases of his character and conduct.

Shelley, as Swinburne said of William
Blake, was born into the church of rebels;
he was born, also, gentle, loving, and fear-
less. The dangers to which such a natural endowment would inevitably expose him
were aggravated by a misguided education,
and by the temper of that feverish and ill-
regulated age in which modern reform began. He was in early years first of all a
revolter; he would do only what seemed to
him best, and in the way which seemed to
him best; he took nothing upon authority,
he acknowledged no validity in the customs
and beliefs which past experience had be-
queathed to men; he must examine every
conclusion anew, and accept or reject it by
the light of his own limited thought and observation; he carried the Protestant spirit
to its ultimate extreme — all legal and intellectual results embodied in institutions or
in accepted beliefs must show cause to him
why they should exist. He was, moreover,
in haste; he could not rest in a doubt, he
could not suspend his judgment, he could
not wait for fuller knowledge. Finding
only incomplete or incompetent answers to
his questioning, he leaped to the conclusion
that there was no answer. Had he been

contented with allowing this spirit to influence only his own private creed and conduct,
mischief enough was sure to be wrought for
him, error and suffering were in store for
him in no common degree. But he was not
merely building an ideal of life and formulating a rule of living for himself; he had,
as he afterward confessed, a passion for reforming the world. He was early in print,
and aspired to teach the world before he
was well out of his teens, — took in his
hands, indeed, the regeneration of Ireland
through pamphlets, and public eloquence,
and personal agitation and supervision. It
is easy to dismiss this as the foolish conceit
of a boy of talent much given to dreaming.
It is easy, too, to dismiss his exile from his
home and his expulsion from Oxford as
childish obstinacy, disobedience, ingratitude,
and presumption; but if there was anything
of these faults in him there was also much
more made evident in these first trials of his
character: there was the capacity for sacrifice, the resolution to be faithful to the truth
as he saw it. The beginning of manhood
found him in the full sway of immature
conviction, and already suffering the penalty.
It is not necessary to follow out in detail

the development of a life so entered upon.
It led him to attack Christianity and to disregard the law of marriage, and this is the
sum and substance of his offense. Yet no
sign, perhaps, is so indicative of the increased liberality of religion in our time as
the attempt which has been made to show
that Shelley was essentially Christian, an
attempt so common and vigorous that Trelawney felt called upon to protest against
it. In this spirit Mr. Symonds writes from
one extreme: " It is certain that as Christianity passes beyond its mediæval phase,
and casts aside the husk of outworn dogmas,
it will more and more approximate to Shelley's exposition. Here, and here only, is a
vital faith adapted to the conditions of modern thought, indestructible because essential,
and fitted to unite instead of separating
minds of divers quality "; and Rev. F. W.
Robertson, from the other extreme, writes:
" I cannot help feeling that there was a
spirit in poor Shelley's mind which might
have assimilated with the spirit of his Re-
deemer, — nay, which I will dare to say was
kindred with that spirit, if only his Re-
deemer had been differently imaged to him.
. . . I will not say that a man who by his

opposition to God means opposition to a demon, to whom the name of God in his mind is appended, is an enemy of God; . . . change the *name* and I will bid that *character* defiance with you!" A candid examination must show, however, that Trelawney is right; there is no doubt that Shelley rejected altogether what is properly known as Christianity, in youth violently and with hatred, while in later years he came to care less about it. At the same time it is to be remembered that he had seen Christianity only in those forms whose most prominent characteristic is defect in charity and love, which Shelley believed to be the central virtues. Probably he never dissociated the Christian God from the Jewish Jehovah, and his feeling towards him is well illustrated in the terrible indictment he makes against him in reference to Milton's delineation of Satan as one " who, in the cold security of undoubted triumph, inflicts upon his fallen enemy the most horrible punishment, not from any mistaken hope of thereby reforming him, but with the avowed purpose of exasperating him to deserve new torments." It is, therefore, impossible to deny Shelley's atheism; the most that can be con-

tended for is that in natural piety, in purity
of life and motive, in conscientious and unselfish action, Shelley was exceptionally conspicuous.

It is here that the second charge against
Shelley has its place. How, it is indignantly
asked, was he unselfish, loving, and conscientious, when he left his youthful wife to
circumstances which resulted in her suicide,
and transferred his devotion to another?
Nothing more can be done than to point out
the fact that Shelley acted in harmony with
his convictions of social duty ; that the first
marriage was the result of knight-errantry
rather than affection, and had become destitute of any pleasure ; that Shelley did not
desert his wife in such a way as to make
her suicide chargeable to him.   These considerations do not, it is true, relieve him of
condemnation, or remove the really great defect in his moral perception of the responsi-
bility which rested upon him in consequence
of a thoughtless and foolish marriage.   Yet
it is not doubtful that in his life he atoned
for his error, if suffering is atonement ; from
that time a shadow fell upon him which
never was removed.   It is hard to find heart
for reproach when one, whose whole gospel

was love, is so cruelly entangled in the un-
foreseen consequences of his acts that he
seems to have wrought the work of hatred.

What, then, under this presentation of
the case, remains to be said for that ideal
character which those who love Shelley believe to have been his possession? That,
beginning life with a theory which left every
desire and impulse free course, which im-
posed no restrictions except those of his
own honor and self-respect, which acknowledged no command not proceeding from his
own reason, he yet served the truth he saw
with entire loyalty and sincerity of heart;
that, making many errors throughout a darkened life, he did not strive by lightness of
heart or logical sophistication to avoid their
penalties of misery and remorse, but kept
them in memory and bore his burden of sorrow courageously; that by intense thought
and bitter experience he came at last to
find the laws of life and to obey them. He
found how impossible it is for the individual to solve the problems put before him, so
that he himself grew content to leave many
of these in doubt; found how ignorant it
was in him to make his own experience the
measure of the conditions of general human

life, and attempt to reform the world's motives and standards by reference to that experience alone; found how little the individual counts for in life, so that the youth, who with fervid hope took up the regeneration of a whole nation in confidence, came to doubt whether it was worth while for him to write at all, and rated himself far below his friend Byron. These characteristics are the evidence of his strength, sincerity, and rightness of purpose; and through these he worked out an ideal of life and rule of living, which differed much from those of his early days. No ideal intrinsically more powerful in influence or more exalted in virtue has been worked out by men who, like himself, found the old familiar standards rationally inadequate and morally weak. These are the essential elements in Shelley's career, and to them his personal qualities and his daily life give form and color. This, too, is the work of a man framed for self-destruction, against whom circumstances did their worst throughout. The marvel is, not that his life was so broken in private happiness, and his public work so unequal in the worth of its results, but, taking all into account, that he saved so much of his life and work through his perception of the valuable objects of living, and his clinging to them.

This, too, was the result of the imperfect years of preparation. He had given him only the traditional thirty years which belong to every genius for trial and training before the finished work can be required. He had just recognized the conditions to which he must conform, and was only ready to begin when he died.

II. HIS ACQUAINTANCES.

It is impossible to condense Shelley's Life in a clear way. One turns the pages, and owns for the thousandth time the fascination of Shelley, from the first glimpse of the boy, pressing his face against the window-pane to kiss his sister, to the hot July afternoon when he made his last embarkation, and the summer storm swept the gleaming mountains from his sight; but no art transmits the spell, and the story, clasped between these periods, must be left in its integrity. Shelley lived in solitude, and died before he was thirty years old; but his career involved such variety of scenes, persons, and incidents, was so thick-strewn with interesting episodes, and contained so many perplexed passages,

that it is a study by itself, and requires
for its mastery an acquaintance with an extensive literature of its own. It were useless
to attempt a criticism, or to describe Shelley
anew, but some unstudied remarks upon his
fortunes in life may be ventured upon.

Must one incur the charge of being supercilious and aristocratic if he acknowledges
at once a feeling, after reading Shelley's life,
of having been in very disagreeable company? Assuredly no one can rise from the
perusal with a heightened respect for human
nature, apart from Shelley. He was born a
gentleman; his innate courtesy clothes him
with attractiveness, and distinguishes him
among his associates as a person of a different kind from them, in his actions and bearing; and the deference which Byron showed
to him, it is not unlikely, sprang from a
perception of this strain of breeding in him
rather than from appreciation of his genius
or his nature. In his earliest fellowship with
school‑friends, for whom he had a kindly
regard at Eton and after they went down
together to Oxford, though Hogg plainly obscures it, there is a gleam here and there of
natural and equal companionship; but this
morning ray soon dies out. He was, after-

wards, almost uniformly unfortunate in his acquaintances. His life was truly one long and sorrowful disillusion; and in it not the least part was the discovery of how he had been deceived in his judgment of persons.

Hogg was his first example. Shelley became familiar with him at Oxford, and, not content with having him for a bosom friend, wished to make him his brother-in-law. At that time Shelley was in the first crude ferment of his intellectual life, eagerly absorbing the new knowledge which came to him from his indiscriminate reading, and disputing on all the usual topics with vehement and unwearied earnestness, insatiable curiosity, and the delight of a youth who has just made the discovery that he has a mind of his own. His thoughts and letters were mostly polemical; ideal elements of morality were growing up in him, and radical views of conduct getting a hold in his convictions. He was willful, precipitate, and heedless through inexperience; he was thrown the more upon himself, and given a violent turn toward rebellion, to which he was prone enough, by his expulsion from Oxford, and the senseless attempt of his family to make him suppress his mental and moral life by denying his first dear conclusions. In this state, partly from adventure and restlessness, perhaps, but also from a sense of obligation, the desire to spread his gospel, and by the mere favor of circumstances, he married his first wife, though he knew that his sympathies were more engaged than his heart.

At Edinburgh, whither the pair had gone, Hogg joined them, and with him they returned to York, where Shelley left his wife in his friend's care during a brief necessary absence. Hogg, who appears to have been not so pure as might be wished in his university days, tried to seduce her; and when Shelley came back he learned the facts. He loved Hogg; he was ashamed, he wrote, to tell him how much he loved him; he was grateful to him for having stood by him and shared his expulsion from the college; and he placed the most extravagant estimate upon his abilities. What followed upon the disclosure Shelley himself tells in a letter written at the time : —

" We walked to the fields beyond York. I desired to know fully the account of this affair. I heard it *from him*, and I believe he was sincere. All I can recollect of that terrible day was that I pardoned him, — fully, freely pardoned him; that I would still be a friend to him, and hoped soon to convince him how lovely virtue was; that his crime, not himself, was the object of my detestation; that I value a human being not for what it has been, but for what it is; that I hoped the time would come when he would regard his horrible error with as much disgust as I did. He said little; he was pale, terror-struck, remorseful."

One may smile at this episode, if he be cynical, and has left youth far enough behind; but for all that, there is something pathetic in these sentences of boyish goodness, this simple belief in the moral principles which Shelley had found in his first search, and to which he had given the allegiance of his unworn heart; and in this scene of forgiveness, still confused with the emotions of first friendship betrayed, one perceives the Shelley we know, though he was not yet out of his teens. Some time elapsed before Shelley realized all the incident meant; then he wrote, "I leave him to his fate;" and when they met again in London, the old footing was gone forever.

Godwin, too, affords a capital example of

a shattered ideal. He was the Socrates of the young poet, and Shelley, who derived the main articles of his political and social creed from the radical philosopher's great book, was already adoring him as one in the pantheon of the immortal dead, when he learned from Southey that his master and emancipator still walked the earth. He sat down at once and wrote a characteristic epistle, in which he expressed himself with the enthusiasm of a disciple not yet twenty, and respectfully but earnestly besought the living friendship and advice of him whom he regarded as the light of the new age. Godwin was interested, and long and frequent letters, admirable in tone upon both sides, passed between them. The elder endeavored to check the irrepressible activity and eager plans of the young reformer, who had no notion of waiting until he should grow old before setting to work to remake society; and the youth, on his part, exhibited a deference and willingness to be guided such as he never showed before or afterwards. The first modification of Shelley's idea of Godwin came in consequence of their personal acquaintance, as was natural; but in discovering that Godwin was really an idiosyncratic mortal, as well as an illuminating intellect, Shelley did not yield his admiration for the sage. One can still see the unbounded astonishment of the poet, which Mary Godwin describes, when she told him her father was annoyed by his addressing him as "Mr." instead of "Esq.," in directing his letters. They got on very well together, however, until Shelley ran away with Mary, — a practical exposition of Godwin's doctrines, which he, having now grown respectable and socially cautious, did not at all relish. Shelley had before this aided Godwin somewhat in financial embarrassments. That philosopher was always in debt; and the young disciple, who, though the heir to a great property, had no way of realizing anything from it except by selling post-obit bonds, agreed with his master that philosophers have a paramount claim on any money their friends might own. He was willing to discharge his duty by getting Godwin out of debt, or assisting him as far as he could in the matter. When he returned to England with Mary he found that the philosopher would not see or forgive him, and positively declined to correspond except upon the subject of how much money

Shelley could. give him. Shelley had no
thought of not doing his own duty, because
of the conduct of other people; and while
he felt Godwin's hardness and inconsistency,
nevertheless he would relieve that great mind
from the little annoyances consequent on
borrowing money without providing means
of repayment.   He, however, was not blind;
and what he learned of Godwin in the course
of these transactions had a destroying influence upon that ideal of the man which he
had formed in his first days of revolutionary
hope.   In the second year of his life with
Mary he told the philosopher what he
thought of the whole matter in a letter which
one may be excused for reading with peculiar satisfaction : —

" It has perpetually appeared to me to
have been your especial duty to see that, so
far as mankind value your good opinion, we
were dealt justly by, and that a young family, innocent and benevolent and united,
should not be confounded with prostitutes
and seducers.   My astonishment, and, I will
confess, when I have been treated with most
harshness and cruelty by you, my indignation, has been extreme, that, knowing as you
do my nature, any considerations should

have prevailed on you to have been thus harsh and cruel. I lamented also over my ruined hopes of all that your genius once taught me to expect from your virtue, when I found that for yourself, your family, and your creditors you would submit to that communication with me which you once rejected and abhorred, and which no pity for my poverty or sufferings, assumed willingly for you, could avail to extort. Do not talk of *forgiveness* again to me, for my blood boils in my veins, and my gall rises against all that bears the human form, when I think of what I, their benefactor and ardent lover, have endured of enmity and contempt from you and from all mankind."

The writer was that youth of twenty-three years, of whom Godwin remarks that he knew "that Shelley's temper was occasionally fiery, resentful, and indignant." It is true that it was so, and one is pleased to find upon what fit occasions it broke out. Shelley, however, had undertaken a hopeless and endless task in trying to extricate Godwin from debt, and he spent much money, raised at a great sacrifice, in the vain attempt. What he thought of these transactions, when his judgment had matured, we know from another delightfully plain-spoken letter, written five years later, in answer to renewed importunities : —

" I have given you the amount of a considerable fortune, and have destituted myself, for the purpose of realizing it, of nearly four times the amount. Except for the *good-will* which this transaction seems to have produced between you and me, this money, for any advantage it ever conferred on you, might as well have been thrown into the sea. Had I kept in my own hands this £4,000 or £5,000, and administered it in trust for your permanent advantage, I should indeed have been your benefactor. The error, however, was greater in the man of mature age, extensive experience, and penetrating intellect than in the crude and impetuous boy. Such an error is seldom committed twice."

But long before this, Shelley, though his estimate of Godwin's powers, in common with that of the people of the time, remained extravagant, had found out the difference between the author of Political Justice and Plato and Bacon.

If any one wonders at the extent to which Shelley let himself be fleeced by the philo-

sophical radical of Skinner Street, he should
reserve some astonishment for the remainder
of the shearers.   Shelley, it is to be remembered, was never in possession of his property, and had only a small allowance at first,
and a thousand pounds a year after he was
twenty-four years old; he was extravagant
in his generosity, and gave money with a
free hand, whenever he had any, to the poor
about him, to his needy friends, and to
causes of one kind and another which ex-
cited in him his passion for philanthropy.
He was, consequently, in his early days,
commonly in debt for his own expenses, and
often in danger of arrest and imprisonment.
When he mentioned his days of poverty, in
that letter to Godwin, it was not a mere
phrase; and though a settlement was at last
made which provided for him sufficiently,
he was never ahead in his savings.   Under
these circumstances, his biography at times
reminds one of the old comedy, with its mob
of parasites and legacy - hunters.   He was
simply victimized by those who could estab-
lish any claim on his benevolence.   No doubt
he gave willingly, with all his heart, to Peacock and Leigh Hunt and the rest, as he did
to Godwin, and thought it was his duty as

well as his pleasure ; but his generosity does not alter the fact that his acquaintances were very dull of conscience in money matters. One begins to relent a little toward Hogg, remembering that he did actually share his own funds with Shelley just after the expulsion from Oxford, when the latter could get no money, owing to his father's displeasure ; and for Horace Smith, the banker, who sometimes advanced money to Shelley, and not too much, one has a feeling of amazed respect.

The worst misfortune of Shelley, however, in the friends he made, was to have met and married Harriet Westbrook. The circumstances of their union and its unlucky course and tragical close have lately been for the first time fully set forth. The marriage on Shelley's side was not originally one of love, but it became one of affection. For two years life went on without the discovery of anything to break the happiness of the pair ; but after the birth of their first child trouble arose, and rapidly culminated. It is most likely that the sister-in-law, Eliza, who lived with them, was the source of the original dissension by her interference, arbitrariness, and control of Harriet ; but, as Shelley had grown in mind and character, the difference between him and his wife in endowment and in taste was bound to make itself felt, and to put an end to the unity of study and spirit of which he had dreamed; and it is clear enough that she had tired of the studies and the purposes in which Shelley's life consisted, and that though overborne for a time, by his influence, she was now showing herself worldly, frivolous, and weak. She had married the heir to a baronetcy and a fortune, and desired to profit by it. In one way and another she had become hard and unyielding toward Shelley, had made him thoroughly miserable, and, in the earlier months of 1814, was living away from him; and he, on his side, as late as May in that year, as appears from stanzas now first printed, was trying to soften her. While affairs were in this condition he first met Mary Godwin, and he fell passionately in love with her, all the more because of the long strain of dejection and loneliness; and in addition to the story of the dissensions that had arisen in his family, and the difference of character and temperament which had declared itself between his wife and himself, Shelley is said to have told Mary that Harriet had been unfaithful to him. If he did not tell her then, he did afterwards. On what evidence he relied we do not know; nor is there any confirmatory proof from other quarters except a letter of Godwin's written after Harriet's suicide, in which he states the same fact as coming from unquestionable authority unconnected with Shelley. Not long before his death Shelley renewed the charge, though in a veiled and inferential way, in a letter to Southey, in which he defends himself for his conduct in this matter, declares his innocence of any harm done or intended, refuses to be held responsible for the suicide of Harriet, and practically asserts that he had grounds for divorce, had he chosen to free himself in that way. There is no need to prove that Shelley was right in his belief of his wife's infidelity; but if it be thought that Shelley did in truth believe her guilty, that has much to do with our estimate of his action. He was twenty-two years old, or nearly that, and he held radical views as to the permanence and sacredness of the marriage bond, as also did Mary, who inherited them from her mother. Their decision to unite their lives, under these circumstances, was a practical admission that Shelley's home was in fact broken up, and that he was free to offer, and Mary to accept, not legal union, but a common home, with the expectation and purpose of complete devotion one to the other, in a pure spirit and for the ordinary ends of marriage.

Shelley did not proceed secretly. He summoned Harriet, who had not thought of such serious results of her action, to London, and told her what he was going to do. She did not consent to the separation, nor does she seem to have regarded it as final. Shelley had a settlement made for her by the lawyers, provided credit for her, and two weeks after the interview left England with Mary. He wrote to Harriet on the journey, assured her of his affection and his care for her, and indulged a plan that she should live near them, which is, perhaps, the most surprising instance of Shelley's purity of mind, and of the unworldliness or unreality, as one chooses to call it, of his conception of how human life might be lived. On his return he saw her, and agreed to leave the children with her; and when his allowance was fixed at a thousand pounds, he gave orders to honor her drafts for two hundred pounds annually.

She had an equal amount from her own family, which had been paid since the beginning of their married life. When Shelley left England the second time, she was thus provided for, one would think, sufficiently. On his return he lost sight of her, and was anxiously inquiring for her, when the news of her suicide reached him. She had put the children, of whom the eldest was three years old, out to board, at a time when he was ill; she had not been permitted to see her father; but the circumstances immediately surrounding her death are not known. Shelley, though he bore his share of natural sorrow for the death of one to whom he had been tenderly attached, did not hold himself guilty of any wrong.

It is no wonder that in the last few years of his life Shelley would not talk of his earlier days, and had a kind of shame in remembering iu what ruin his hopes and purposes and the enthusiasm of his youth had fallen; he felt it as an indignity to the nobleness of spirit which, in spite of all his failures, he knew had been his throughout. As we see those years, it is only for himself that we prize them; and it is a pleasure to be enabled to look on them free from that saddening retrospect of his own mind, and observe how natural and simple he really was. No one has ever had the days of his youth so laid open to the common gaze, and this is one charm of his personality, that we know him as a brother or a friend. The pages afford many happy anecdotes; but one can linger here only to mark the constant playfulness of Shelley, which was a bright element in his earlier career and not altogether absent in his Italian life. The passion for floating paper - boats, which he indulged unweariedly, is well known; but at all times he was ready for sport, and could even trifle with his dearest plans, as in the flotilla of bottles and aerial navy of fire-balloons, all loaded with revolutionary pamphlets, which he sent forth on the Devonshire coast. His running about the little garden, hand in hand with Harriet; his impersonating fabulous monsters with Leigh Hunt's children, who begged him "not to do the horn;" and his favorite sport with his little temporarily adopted Marlow girl, of placing her on the dining-table, and rushing with it across the long room, are instances that readily recur to mind, and illustrate the gayety and high spirits which

really belonged to him, and which perhaps
the Serchio last knew when it bore him and
his boat on his summer-day voyages. This
side of his nature ought to be remembered,
as well as that " occasionally fiery, resentful,
and indignant" quality which Godwin observed, and the intense and restless practi-
cality of the impatient reformer, when one
thinks of Shelley (as he has been too often
represented) as only a morbid, sensitive,
idealizing poet, of a rather feminine spirit.
That portrait of him is untruthful, for he
was of a most masculine, active, and naturally joyful nature.

After he left England for the last time,
and took up his abode in Italy, principally,
it would seem, because of the social reproach and public stigma under which he
lived, and by which he felt deeply wronged,
he was not really much more fortunate in
his company. The immediate reason for
the journey was to take Byron's natural
daughter, Allegra, to her father at Venice ;
the mother, Miss Clairmont, went with them,
and, as it turned out, continued to be a
member of Shelley's family, as she had been
since his union with Mary. It is now known
that the Shelleys were ignorant of the *lia-*

ison, both when it began in London, and afterward when they first met Byron at Geneva; but Shelley had a warm affection for Miss Clairmont, whose friendlessness appealed to his sympathy, and he spent much time in Italy in trying to make Byron do his duty toward Allegra, and to soften the ill-nature of her parents toward each other. Byron's conduct in this matter was a powerful element in generating in Shelley that thorough contempt he expressed for the former as a man. But though Shelley's most winning qualities are to be observed, and his tact was conspicuously called forth by their negotiations in regard to the child, yet the connection with Miss Clairmont was unfortunate. That it repeatedly drew scandal upon him was a minor matter; it was of more consequence that in his family she was a disturbing element, and Mary, who had disliked to have her as an inmate almost from the first, finally insisted on her withdrawal, but not until frequent disagreements had sadly marred the peace of Shelley's home. Mary, indeed, was not perfect, any more than other very young wives; and by her jealousies, and yet more, it seems, by her attempts to make Shelley conform to the world, especially in the last year or two, she tried and harassed him; and so it came about that his love took the form of tenderness for her welfare and feelings, and often of despondency for himself. Miss Clairmont was a source of continual trouble for him in many ways: she was of an unhappy temperament and hard to live with; but with his long-enduring and charitable disposition, and his extraordinary tenacity in attachment, and perfect readiness to admit the least obligation upon him, proceeding from any one in trouble, he never wavered in his devotion to her interests and care for her happiness. It is a curious fact that Miss Clairmont, who lived to be very old, manipulated the written records of this portion of her life, so that her evidence is of very questionable worth, though better, one hopes, than that of her mother, the second Mrs. Godwin, whose lying about the Shelleys was of the most wholesale and conscienceless kind.

As with Miss Clairmont, so in a less degree with others of the Italian circle. But enough has been said of the character of the people whom Shelley knew. It cannot be that they cut so poor a figure because of Shelley's presence, hard as the contrast of

common human nature must be with him.
It is observable, and it is in some sort a test,
that he did not overvalue them. Hogg, Peacock, and Medwin were all deceived, if they
thought he trusted them or held them closer
than mere friendly acquaintances; there is
no evidence that he felt for Williams or
Trelawney any more than an affectionate
good will; toward Leigh Hunt he had the
kindest feeling of gratitude and of respect,
and for Gisborne and Reveley a warm cor-
diality, but nothing more. Mary he loved,
though with full knowledge of her weak-
nesses, in a manly way; for Miss Clairmont
he had a true affection; and he recognized
poetically a womanly attractiveness in Mrs.
Williams, who seems to have represented to
him the spirit of restfulness and peace, in
the last months of his life. But at the end,
his errors respecting men and things being
swept away, his ideals removed into the
eternal world, and his disillusion complete,
the most abiding impression is of the loneliness in which he found himself; and remembering this, one forgets the companions he
had upon his journey, and fastens attention
more closely upon the man through whose
genius that journey has become one of un-
dying memory.

There is no thought of eulogizing him in saying that he represents the ideal of personal and social aspiration, of the love of beauty and of virtue equally, and of the hope of eradicating misery from the world ; hence springs in large measure his hold on young hearts, on those who value the spirit above all else and do not confine their recognition of it within too narrow bounds, and on all who are believers in the reform of the world by human agencies. He represents this ideal of aspiration in its most impassioned form ; and in his life one reads the saddest history of disillusion. It is because, in the course of this, he abated no whit of his life-long hope, did not change his practice of virtue, and never yielded his perfect faith in the supreme power of love, both in human life and in the universe, that his name has become above all price to those over whom his influence extends. It is, perhaps, more as a man than as a poet merely that he is beloved ; the shadows upon his reputation, as one approaches nearer, are burnt away in light ; and he is the more honored, the more he is known. For it would be wrong to close even these informal remarks without expressing dissent from the assumption that

Shelley's intellectual and moral life was one long mistake. Disillusion it was, and the nature of it has been indicated by the single point of his acquaintances ; but a life of disillusion and one of mere mistake are not to be confounded together. Better fortune cannot be asked for a youth than that he should conceive life nobly, and, in finding wherein it falls short, should yet not fall short himself of his ideal beyond what may be forgiven to human frailty. Shelley's misconceptions were the conditions of his living the ideal life at all, and differed from those of other youths in face of an untried world only by their moral elevation, passion, and essential nobleness ; he matured as other men do by time and growth and experience, and he suffered much by the peculiar circumstances of his fate ; but in the issue the substance of error in his life was less than it seems. Shelley, at least, never admitted he had been wrong in the essential doctrines of his creed and the motives of his acts, though he had been deceived in regard to human nature and what was possible to it in society.

III. HIS ITALIAN LETTERS.

The prose work of Shelley has remained in the obscurity which it once shared with his poetry. The formal essays, which concern the transitory affairs of the world or themes of thought remote through their generality, are valued, even by admirers of Shelley, mainly as *media* of his spirit; the familiar letters, scattered in old books, or collected only in a costly edition, and deprived of literary effectiveness because those of high and enduring interest have never been selected and massed until recently, have escaped any wide public attention; even the translations have been neglected. All this really large body of prose, however exalted by its informing enthusiasm, however exquisite in language, and melodious, lies outside the open pathways of literature. It is this fact which gave the element of surprise to what Mr. Arnold called his doubt " whether Shelley's delightful Essays and Letters, which deserve to be far more read than they are now, will not resist the wear and tear of time better, and finally come to stand higher, than his poetry," — a judgment which well deserved Dr. Garnett's quiet rejoinder that

" this deliverance will be weighed by those
to whose lot it may fall to determine Mr.
Arnold's own place as a critic." Dr. Garnett adds that, in an age when all letters
approximate to the ideal set by men of business, Shelley's alone, among those of his
time, rank with Gray's, Pope's, Cowper's, or
Walpole's in possessing a certain classical
impress similar to that of deliberate artistic
work ; and, secondly, that they exhibit the
mind of the poet as clearly as Marlborough's
do the mind of the general, or Macaulay's
the mind of the man of letters. Their two
prime qualities are beauty of form and transparency.

The sense of form has usually been denied
to Shelley, and if by it is meant the purely
critical impulse to remodel, revise, and polish
for the sake of that finish which the schools
prize, Shelley neither possessed it nor sought
for it with any strong desire, but rather rejected it as dangerously submitting the mind
to system, against which he was prejudiced.
But if by the sense of form is meant the instinct for proportion, for regulated combination, for natural development of sensation
into idea, idea into passion, so that the poem
issues in a single harmony in the mind and

heart; if, in other words, by that loose phrase is meant, not the corrective power of the critical, but the shaping power of the creative faculty working out ideal beauty directly, then both in his brief and in much of his longer poems Shelley was singularly distinguished by it. This spontaneous beauty of form, if we may so phrase it, is the only species that is found in these letters: fitness of words, sweetness of cadence, modulation of feeling in immediate response to thought and image, all conspiring to make up perfection of utterance, are continually present, but not through erasure and elaboration. Shelley's self-training in literature, almost unrivaled as an apprenticeship in its length and continuity, more comprehensive, profound, and ardent than Pope's, more vital than Milton's, had made such literary lucidity and grace the habit of his pen, and he was fortunate in employing his gift upon subjects intrinsically most interesting to cultivated men : upon the art and landscape of Italy, or his own always high human relations, or his poetic moods.

In what he says of statues and paintings he shows but slight knowledge of art. The keenness of his perceptions and the warmth

of his feelings made him particularly open
to sensuous effects, so that in general he
worships the later schools. In painting,
especially, he can hardly be considered a safe
guide for others, because his praise or censure is largely dependent on his temperament for its justification : a picture which is
consonant with his own imagination, and
stirs it, is thereby raised and glorified, but
one whose theme would have been differently developed by himself is at once made
pale by contrast with the quick visions of
his own vividly pictorial mind. Here is a
portion of his description of a Christ Beati-
fied : —

"The countenance is heavy, as it were,
with the rapture of the spirit; the lips
parted, but scarcely parted, with the breath
of intense but regulated passion ; the eyes
are calm and benignant; the whole features
harmonized in majesty and sweetness."

One cannot but feel that the face which
Shelley thus summons up before us bears
the same relation to the original as what the
dull-minded call his plagiarisms from Lodge
do to that poet's lyrics. Shelley often paints
the picture over upon the outlines of the old
canvas; but this transforming or penetrat-

ing power, as it will be differently named just as one believes the given picture to lack or possess what Shelley saw in it, lends such passages not only surpassing beauty, but a real value as interpretations of art. Much as Ruskin would differ from Shelley's judgments, the two are essentially similar in their mode of treatment, and in their faculty of giving the equivalent of form and color in eloquence.

The description of landscape, which is another principal topic, possesses even more plainly classic beauty. Whether Shelley writes of nature in her wild and picturesque scenes, or where the presence of man has added pathos or dignity to her loveliness; whether he flashes the view upon us in one perfect line, or unfolds it slowly iu unconfused detail, he displays the highest power in this field of literature. This view from the Forum of Pompeii, which, instead of being robed with " the gray veil of his own words," seems filled with " the purple noon's transparent light," cannot be surpassed as speech at once familiar and noble : —

" At the upper end, supported on an elevated platform, stands the temple of Jupiter. Under the colonnade of its portico we sate, and pulled out our oranges, and figs, and bread, and medlars, — sorry fare, you will say, — and rested to eat. Here was a magnificent spectacle. Above and between the multitudinous shafts of the sun-shining columns was seen the sea, reflecting the purple noon of heaven above it, and supporting, as it were, on its line the dark, lofty mountains of Sorrento, of a blue inexpressibly deep, and tinged toward their summits with streaks of new-fallen snow. Between was one small green island. To the right was Capreæ, Inarime, Prochyta, and Misenum. Behind was the single summit of Vesuvius, rolling forth volumes of thick white smoke, whose foam-like column was sometimes darted into the clear dark sky, and fell in little streaks along the wind. Between Vesuvius and the nearer mountains, as through a chasm, was seen the main line of the loftiest Apennines to the east. The day was radiant and warm. Every now and then we heard subterranean thunder of Vesuvius; its distant, deep peals seemed to shake the very air and light of day, which interpenetrated our frames with the sullen and tremendous sound."

Thus he wrote when merely passive to

nature's influences; but when he begins to think he irradiates the scene; he lifts it with his aspiration and softens it with his regret; he brings it near by reminiscences of the English fields and cliffs and streams; he informs it with the large interests of the intellectual life; and not infrequently he concludes with a passage which, in the arrangement of its images, the sequence of its thought and feeling, the unity of its effect, in all except metrical structure, is a poem. Many paragraphs might be cited which show the character of his genius as directly as do his verses, and which justify the claim advanced for them as having the permanent interest of ideal beauty.

The principal charm of these letters, however, as Dr. Garnett says, is not artistic, but moral. It is not meant to refer by this term to the practical morality of Shelley's deeds, or to his conscientiousness, humanity, self-sacrifice, or other such qualities as they are here displayed; of these there is no longer need to speak. Nor is it meant simply to express the gratification one feels at finding that Shelley, unlike many men of letters who disappoint us by being only common mortals in private life, never falls

below our conception of him, indicative as it
is of his purity that his "unpremeditated
song" does not fail to reach the height of
his great argument. What impresses one
most is rather the character of the life itself, of the mind to which "trust in all
things high came natural," that moved with
equal ease among the things of beauty, on
the heights of thought, or amid the common
and trivial cares of household life and in
the offices of friendship, and knew no difference in the level of his life, so single was
his nature and so completely expressed in
all he did. In the most ideal passages, in
those most impersonal, one does not lose the
sense of friendliness in them, of the sweet
human relationship which underlies the tell-
ing of what he has to say, and keeps the
letters in their appropriate sphere. They
are not rhapsodies, or soliloquies, or dis-
quisitions; in other words, the visitations of
the spirit that came to Shelley, and left
record of themselves in this beauty and eloquence and imaginative passion, did not iso-
late him even momentarily, and could not
sever him from his friends. Who these
were, we know well enough: Miss Hitche-
ner, the blue-stocking; Hogg, the betrayer;

the Williamses and Gisbornes, who seem to have belonged to the class of people known as satisfying; Peacock, who, with all his nympholepsy, was a born beef-eater; Smith, the obliging; Hunt, the " wren," and Byron, the " eagle," in Shelley's nomenclature, — the too fortunate people who knew Shelley and whom he loved. They formed the environment, which needs to be kept in mind by any who would estimate Shelley's moral power; amid them he lived his high life and made it theirs, in the case of the most, during their communion with him. In a vague analogical way he sometimes brings to mind the Greek gods, who, with all their divine attributes of beauty, power, dignity, were singular among deities for their companionableness; Shelley had that divine quality of being familiar and retaining his original brightness. Toward Byron alone does he show any repulsion; he recognized Byron's admirable qualities, but he was alienated by the latter's selfishness, worldliness, and earthliness, even while he kept terms of amity. Shelley's sentence on Byron is most serious evidence against him, and it is now supported by much that Shelley could not have known; but it need not be discussed here.

It is especially fortunate that the letters exhibit him after his boyhood, with its false starts, its follies and prejudices, its narrowness and confusion, was passed; of that time we get only a noble echo in his sad remembrance, amid his seeming failure, of the lofty purpose with which he had entered life, while we see the depth unconfused by the tumult of his soul. In these last years, it is true, the thwarting of his practical instinct was ending in hopelessness; but if the earthly paradise that was the faith of his youth was now fading away, he was lifting his eyes to the city in the heavens, and had acknowledged the vanity of seeking the ideal he knew, except in the eternal; he had worked out his salvation. Perhaps after all we do wrong to lament his death; with that tragedy, in which every thought of Shelley involuntarily concludes, his work as a quickener of the spirit was accomplished. More finished works of art he might have given to us; he could not have left a nobler or more enkindling memory. These letters help in the still necessary labor of clearing away the misconceptions concerning him. In them one sees him only in the quiet of his soul, and will come to a better knowledge and perhaps a higher truth concerning him than is possible by reading his changeful poems alone.

SOME ACTORS' CRITICISMS OF OTHELLO, IAGO, AND SHYLOCK.

An actor of genius, at the moment of impersonating (either in imagination or in fact) a character of Shakespeare's, is probably nearer to the dramatist's creative mood than any one else can get, except possibly the poet born. He may, to use a phrase of Booth's, in speaking of this mode of coming to an understanding of Shakespeare, " hit it " by the mere force within that bears him naturally on. Or, to take the case in which his sympathy with the *rôle* is imperfect, he may perceive wherein he is defective more clearly by his conscious failure than by any analysis. Again, the difficulties that arise from not knowing how Shakespeare put the play on the stage may not be solved rightly, it is true, by the moderns ; but the conclusions of the acting fraternity on these matters are much more worthy of weight than those of men unacquainted with the practical working of that " business " which is a sort of cement for the scenes. Support could be found from many quarters for what Dr. Furness says in behalf of actors as useful critics; but without further reasoning, one may invite attention to some considerations in regard to Othello suggested by quotations from memoirs of the profession and other records, and especially from Booth's annotated acting-copy, extracts from which, although not made with any view to publication, may be found in the Variorum edition of the play.

Mr. White, in his satirical essay upon The Acting of Iago, expresses the opinion that all the modern impersonations are inadequate, and that the fault springs from a radical misconception of the character. Theatrical companies are made up, every one knows, with an actor for each of the varieties of human nature which are usual in a play; so far as character is concerned, they enact types. Iago, of course, falls to the lot of the " heavy villain," whose aim, in stage life, is to do his wickedest always, everywhere, and in as many guises as possible; he is continually pointing to the mark of Cain on his forehead, so that there shall

be no mistake about his identity. "I think,"
says Booth,—and the criticism holds all
the meat of Mr. White's essay in a nutshell,
—"the light comedian should play the villain's part, not the 'heavy man;' I mean
the Shakespearean villains." In consonance
with this is his reiterated advice to his Iago
to think evil all the time, but not to show
it; to be the prince of good fellows, inexhaustible in *bonhomie*, genial, jovial, gentle-
manly,—the friend and pleasant companion
whom every one liked, whom Desdemona
trifled with, and Cassio respected for his
soldiership, and Othello trusted as a man as
faithful in love as he was wise in the world.
"A certain bluffness," Booth says "(which
my temperament does not afford), should
be added to preserve the military flavor of
the character: in this particular I fail utterly; my Iago lacks the soldierly quality."
So far, certainly, Booth does not differ from
Mr. White in his conception of the bearing,
the outward manner and sensible aspect, of
the Venetian liar. Let us look at it from
Mr. White's point of view: " Edwin Booth's
Iago is not externally a mere hardened villain, but a super-subtle Venetian, who works
out his devilish plans with a dexterous light-

ness of touch and smooth sinuosity of movement that suggest the transmigration of a
serpent into human form. And in his vis-
age, and, above all, in his eye, burns the
venom of his soul. . . . But even Edwin
Booth's Iago, although much finer and more
nearly consistent with itself and with the
facts of the tragedy than any other that is
known to the annals of the stage, is not the
Iago that Shakespeare drew." But what is
it that is lacking? Mr. White paints Iago
as the popular flatterer, the sympathetic
sycophant, the gay, easy-going, pleased, and
pleasing fellow; and, so far as the side
shown to the world is concerned, this is
Booth's conception, and (allowing for the
defect of soldier - like frankness which he
feels in himself) it is his impersonation.
Why is it not, then, Shakespeare's Iago?
Mr. White is ready with his answer: Because Shakespeare's Iago would do no harm,
except to advance his fortunes; he had no
malice; he was merely selfish, utterly unscrupulous as to his means of obtaining what
he sought, ready to win his gain at any ruin.
Now, it is clear that the evil which Mr.
White has just said burns in the actor's eye
is not mere selfishness, not the cold light of

calculation simply, with no more rooted passion ; it is just what Mr. White says Iago did not have,—it is malice. So one gets the hint ; and on searching the remarks of Booth to see what indications there are of his conception of the essence of Iago's soul, the spring of his motive, the changing emotions that enveloped his thoughts at their birth, one perceives at once that, while Booth would have Iago outwardly amiable, he has not the least idea of reducing the dye of villainy in which the character has been steeped by those of old time. Inside, Booth· has no doubt, Iago was a spirit of hate, and he knows at what moments of anxious interest, at what crises of the temptation and the plotting, this will gleam out in the expression of the eye, or in those slight tell-tale changes which are natural to the most self-possessed man, and are significant to us only because we are on the watch for them. By observing, consequently, with what passages he connects this devilish malignancy of nature in Iago, one can judge, as between him and Mr. White, what justification he has for making Iago cruel as well as selfish, and revengeful as well as ambitious. Mr. White's theory is that Iago wished to supplant Cassio, and ruined Desdemona in order to accomplish this end ; that he used his suspicion of Othello's intimacy with his wife almost as an after-thought, to bolster up his purpose with an excuse ; and that, having chosen his method with perfect indifference to its morality or its humanity, he overreached himself and failed. This view may gain upon one by its plausible and emphatic setting forth, just as pleas for Judas Iscariot or any other client of a clever devil's advocate may do, but only momentarily ; for when one attempts to adjust the speeches of Iago, word by word and line by line, to this conception, especially with such notes of direction and caution as these of Booth's to the actor, echoing the text, as they do, through all modulations of suspicion, suspense, and suppressed passion, the idea of an Iago without malice simply dissolves, and leaves not a rack behind. In reality, this new notion of Mr. White's is only the old story that Iago is motiveless, which has disturbed so many critics, and given occasion to such marvelous explanations of his villainy. The disparity between the moral causes and the mortal results, between the errors and the penalties of the victims, has been widely felt; the attempt is consequently made to ascribe a cause for the catastrophe that shall justify it to the reason; and naturally one writer has over-accented and exaggerated one element in the play, and a second writer another element, and so on; but Mr. White bears away the palm from all in his assertion that Iago did all the mischief just to get on in the world, and that the only reason it was so great was because of the unlimited power for harm in the union of ability to flatter with utter unscrupulousness in a man's make-up. Shakespeare gives the key-note of the action in the very first words Iago utters, unheard except by his own bosom. What was the first thought on his lips then? " I hate the Moor." And perhaps in that most difficult moment of the *rôle*, the climax of Iago's fate, the elder Booth was right in making the expression of this intense enmity dominant in " the Parthian look which Iago, as he was borne off, wounded and in bonds, gave Othello, — a Gorgon stare, in which hate seemed both petrified and petrifying." In this matter the actors seem to carry it over the editor, who, indeed, was in that essay a better social satirist than Shakespearean scholar; and, to our mind, the conception of Mr. White is too inharmonious, also, with the intellectual power and the delight in its exercise so marked in Shakespeare's and in Booth's Iago.

There is more scope for different interpretations in Othello's case than in Iago's. Othello, it is obvious to any one of the least insight, is a character in whom temperament counts for so much more than anything else as practically to possess the whole man; his actions proceed directly from his nature; his doubts and suspicions act at once upon his heart, and are converted into emotion of the most simple and primitive type almost instantaneously; his mental agony itself tends to become blind physical suffering; he does not think, — he feels. It is in the expression of temperament that the actor is left most free by the dramatist, is least shackled by words, and oftenest relies upon other modes of utterance, among which (we too easily forget) language is only one. In Othello, consequently, who is the creature of his temperament, the actor influences the character to an unusual degree; and as the range of feeling is from the lowest notes of tender happiness to the explosions of unlimited despair, the way in which the actor conceives of feeling, his ideas of what makes it noble, and of the manner in which a grand nature would express it, affect the play profoundly. A certain bent has been given to the stage interpretation and also to criticism, by the notion that Shakespeare meant to exhibit in Othello a barbaric passion, the boiling up of a savage nature, the Oriental fervor and rashness, the dæmon of the Moorish race. Yet nothing is plainer in Shakespeare than his utter disregard of historical accuracy; he never depicted a race type, except the Jewish. If Theseus is an Athenian, or Coriolanus or Cæsar himself a Roman, then Othello may be a Moor; but it is most conformable to the facts to regard them all as simply ideal men, who take from their circumstances a color of nationality and a place in time, but who are essentially all of one race. The view of those actors who give Othello a ferocity of emotion because he is a Moor, or of those critics who discern in the violence and brute unreason of some players in this part something to praise on the score of Othello's birth under a hot Mauritanian sun deserves no sympathy. The

Oriental touch in the impersonation ought not to go beyond such slight signs and tokens as the crescent scimiter, — of which Booth says, "It is harmless," — if we are to keep to Shakespeare's art as something better than a costumer's. Othello does not exhibit one extravagance that requires to be excused by the reflection that it is natural to an alien race, though not to the English. But within the limits of the character conceived as merely ideal, there is a fine opportunity for difference among actors, and they have availed themselves of it. To indicate it by a word, Othello's passion seems to have been the cardinal thought of Kean, irresistible, compulsive as "the Pontick Sea," impressive by its main force and elemental sweep; Fechter, whose conception of nobleness of nature was a poor one, sank all the heroic in the melodrama to which the situations lent themselves; and Booth, giving far more distinctness to Othello's suffering, so that his revenge becomes hardly more than an incident in the course of his own soul's torture, reveals the scene of the tragedy at once as in Othello's breast, where the spirit of evil is feeding on a mighty but guileless heart. It is not Desdemona's death that

is the climax, — that is mere pity ; but
the tragic element finds its conclusion in
Othello's last speech and stroke. The intensity of Kean or the ideality of Booth,
working upon the tragic temperament in
each, must produce Othello with a difference : one tempts to excess in ferocity, the
other in pathos ; but either is consistent with
the text. After all, it is with great actors
as with poets, — their creations partake of
their own nature, in all heroic and ideal
parts ; but if, as is thought, sympathy is the
best revealer of the inner meaning of works
of the imagination, certainly the disciplined
and habitual enacting of great *rôles* by actors of genius ought to be a source of light
and knowledge regarding them, notwithstanding the allowance that is to be made
for the " personal error " of individuality.

It is a striking quality in the immortality
of The Merchant of Venice that it has survived a change in the public mind in its attitude toward the Jewish people. To the
Elizabethans, and Shakespeare among them,
the Jew was hateful. It may well be questioned to what extent Shakespeare himself,
with all the tolerance that his understanding

of the springs of human nature gave him, felt the pity in the dramatic situation of Shylock that a modern audience must feel. Booth's conception of Shakespeare's creation is too direct and natural not to justify itself to the student, — "'an inhuman wretch, incapable of pity, void and empty from any dram of mercy.' It has been said that he was an affectionate father and a faithful friend. When, where, and how does he manifest the least claim to such commendation? Tell me that, and unyoke! 'T was the money value of Leah's ring that he grieved over, not its association with her, else he would have shown some affection for her daughter, which he did not or she would not have called her home 'a hell,' robbed and left him. Shakespeare makes her do these un‑Hebrew things to intensify the baseness of Shylock's nature. If we side with him in his self-defense, 't is because we have charity, which he had not; if we pity him under the burden of his merited punishment, 't is because we are human, which he is not, except in shape, and even that, I think, should indicate the crookedness of his nature." Booth goes on to justify this traditional conception by an easy argument against the notion of "the heroic Hebrew," the type of the vengeance of a persecuted race, whose wrongs justify its acts. He refers to the "dangerous 'bit of business'" when Shylock whets his knife. "Would the heroic Hebrew have stooped to such a paltry action? No, never, in the very white-heat of his pursuit of vengeance! But vengeance is foreign to Shylock's thought; 't is revenge he seeks, and he gets just what all who seek it get, — 'sooner or later,' as the saying is."

This characterization is not too vigorous, nor does it go too far. We may find it not only in Shylock as Shakespeare drew him, but reflected also from Antonio. It is in Antonio personally that the attitude of the mediæval Christian toward the Jew is found. The unexplained melancholy of Antonio, his fidelity in high-minded friendship, and the dignity of his bearing under the cruelty to which he is exposed have obscured to us the other side of his character as the Rialto merchant. We see more of Bassanio's Antonio than of Shylock's: the man who had interfered with the usurer in every way and personally maltreated him, and was as like to do the same again; the proud, hard-hearted, and insulting magnifico whom Shylock hated for himself.   Antonio is every whit as heartless to the Jew in the hour of his triumph as Shylock was to him when the balance leaned the other way.   His cruelty is lacking only in the physical element; it is not bloody, but it goes to the bone and marrow of Shylock's nature none the less. There is no sign that Shakespeare saw any wrong in all this.   It was thus that the Christians looked upon the Jews, and they thought such treatment right.   Shakespeare differed from others — from Marlowe, for example, in his delineation of the Jew at Malta — in one point only: he was able to take Shylock's point of view, to understand his motives, to assign the reasons with which revenge justified its own motions; in a word, to represent Shylock's humanity.   The speeches he puts into the Jew's mouth are intense and eloquent expressions of the reasoning of that "lodged hate" in his bosom; they are true to fact and to nature; on our ears they come with overwhelming force, and it is impossible to our thoughts that Shakespeare could have written them without sympathy for the wrongs that they set forth with such fiery heat.   But when from this it is argued that Shakespeare, in writing this play, made a deliberate plea for toleration, and carried it as far as the necessities of his plot and the temper of his times permitted, then it is needful to remind ourselves of what Booth calls " the baseness of Shylock's nature." Shakespeare did represent him as base, with avarice, cunning, and revenge for the constituent elements of his character; he did not hesitate to let the exhibition of these low qualities approach the farcical, as he would never have done had he thought of the Jew as in any sense heroic. Shylock had suffered insult and wrong, but there was nothing in him individually to excite commiseration. From beginning to end he shows no noble quality. Modern sympathy with him, apart from the pity that tragedy necessarily stirs, is social sympathy, not personal; it is because he is an outcast and belongs to an outcast race, because every man's hand is against him and against all his people, that the audience of this century perceives an injustice inherent in his position itself, antecedent to, and independent of, any of his acts; and this injustice is ignored in the play. The feeling which Shylock, as a person, excites, and should excite, is nearer that which Lady Martin describes as her experience: " I have always felt in the acting that my desire to find extenuations for Shylock's race and for himself leaves me,.and my heart grows almost as stony as his own. I see his fiendish nature fully revealed. I have seen the knife sharpened to cut quickly through the flesh, the scales brought forward to weigh it; have watched the cruel, eager eyes, all strained and yearning to see the gushing blood welling from the side ' nearest the heart,' and gloating over the fancied agonies and death-pangs of his bitter foe. This man-monster, this pitiless, savage nature, is beyond the pale of humanity; it must be made power-less to hurt. I have felt that with him the wrongs of his race are really as nothing compared with his own remorseless hate. He is no longer the wronged and suffering man ; and I longed to pour down on his head the ' justice ' he has clamored for, and will exact without pity." Upon this matter Spedding admits of no reply. " The best contribution," he says, " which I can offer to this discussion is the expression of an old man's difficulty in accepting these new dis-coveries of profound moral and political designs underlying Shakespeare's choice and treatment of his subjects. I believe he was a man of business, — that his principal business was to produce plays which would draw. . . . But if, instead of looking about for a story to 'please' the Globe audience, he had been in search of a subject under cover of which he might steal into their minds 'a more tolerant feeling toward the Hebrew race,' I cannot think he would have selected for his hero a rich Jewish merchant plotting the murder of a Christian rival by means of a fraudulent contract, which made death the penalty of non-payment at the day, and insisting on the exaction of it. In a modern Christian audience it seems to be possible for a skillful actor to work on the feelings of an audience so far as to make a man engaged in such a business an object of respectful sympathy. But can anybody believe that in times when this would have been much more difficult, Shakespeare would have *chosen* such a case as a favorable one to suggest toleration to a public prejudiced against Jews?"

The omnipresent devil's advocate has several times come to Shylock's defense with a legal plea. Those who could find something to urge in extenuation of Judas Iscariot had an easy task in showing that the Jew of Venice was more sinned against than sinning. The decisions of the young doctor who came armed with the recommendation of the learned Bellario have been overruled in every court of appeal. The bond itself is declared invalid, inasmuch as it contained an immoral proviso in the article that sought Antonio's death; the attempt to defeat it, its validity having once been granted, by denying the right to draw blood and requiring the exact amount of a pound of flesh to be cut out, is characterized as a wretched quibble, and set aside on the ground that a right once allowed carries with it the minor rights to make it effectual; the denial of the original debt for the reason that it had been tendered and refused in open court is declared a gross error, such tender having no other result than to destroy any claim for interest subsequently. But not to mention all the grave reasons alleged to break down the reputation of the Court of Venice and show the illegality of its judgments, it is clear that on legal grounds the case was very badly managed, and in the event the Jew met with no better fortune than was the lot

of his race before an unscrupulous and hos-
tile tribunal everywhere.   Nevertheless, the
disputants upon the other side, who allege the
substantial justice of the decisions rendered,
do well to remove the discussion out of the
plane of legality.   There is much that is
weighty in their argument.   Shylock must
be regarded as standing, after the nature of
Judaism, for the law as a thing of the letter;
this is the justice which he demands, not
real, but literal; and if, by a still more
strict interpretation of the letter of the bond
than he had thought of, his claim was de-
feated, the audience will acknowledge the
relevancy of the new point that is made,
and will enjoy the spectacle of the Biter
Bit, in which there is always an element of
comic justice.   As to the quibble involved,
that belongs to the nature of literal interpretation always.   Thus the matter is not
without defense even on this level.   But
what really pleases the audience is not the
method, but the fact, of the Jew's defeat;
and in the fact, however brought about, lies
the ethical element, the victory of real over
illusory justice, of equity over legality, of
the right over the pretense of right.   Shakespeare was not expressly philosophical; but

there is little straining of the facts of the case in the view that in the discomfiture of that "law" which the Jew invoked, in the signal defeat inflicted on the letter of the bond, there is a suggestion of the conflict between Judaism and Christianity, the literal and the spiritual, the law and that justice with its elements of mercy into which the law develops, which is one of the great phases of historical civilization. Whether Shakespeare put it there is immaterial; but that a modern audience finds it there, and that it was at least dimly present to an Elizabethan audience, is hardly to be questioned. The idea is a simple and ancient one; and in it is to be found whatever ethical meaning the play may have.

But it ought to be always remembered that the primary endowment of Shakespeare was the artistic temperament: he was a poet first, and everything else afterwards. To say this is the same thing with saying — though it must be stated briefly — that the ethical principle in him was a necessity of the imagination, not of the understanding; was vision rather than inference; was a part and not the whole. One can no more imagine life truly without ethics than he can

imagine mass without cohesion; a creative
genius, consequently, a man of imagination
all compact, does not necessarily start from
ethics in moulding his works, but it is more
likely that the moral principle which his
works must contain as a part of their reality will be secondary and derivative. Shakespeare is ethical because he imagined life
truly; he did not imagine life truly because
he had thought out, in Lord Bacon's manner, the general principles of morals.

SIR GEORGE BEAUMONT, COLE-RIDGE, AND WORDSWORTH.

Sir George Beaumont appears to have been one of the most agreeable of men. He had not merely high breeding, but humanity of disposition, delightful companionableness, and the refinement that springs from artistic pursuits. Haydon accuses his manners of a want of moral courage. " What his taste dictated to be right, he would shrink from asserting if it shocked the prejudices of others or put himself to a moment's inconvenience," was the fault that this critic had in mind; but this is only to class him with the men who do not think that the truth is always to be spoken in society, and prefer tact to an aggressive egotism. Sir Humphry Davy notices especially that he was a " remarkably *sensible* man, which I mention because it *is* somewhat remarkable in a painter of genius who is at the same time a man of rank and an exceedingly amusing companion." Southey was struck by the apparent happiness of his life, and the absence of any reference to afflictions or anxieties that he might have experienced, and says that he " had as little liking for country sports as for public business of any kind," being absorbed by art and nature ; and, to add Scott's kind words of him in his diary, that excellent judge writes, " Sir George Beaumont 's dead ; by far the most sensible and pleasing man I ever knew. Kind, too, in his nature, and generous, — gentle in society, and of those mild manners which tend to soften the causticity of the general London tone of persiflage and personal satire. I am very sorry — as much as it is in my nature to be — for one whom I could see but seldom." This is a concert of praise which it is a pleasure to associate with the name of the man who was, chiefly, the founder of the National Gallery in Trafalgar Square.

He was a friend of the artists of his time, and a patron of Wilkie and Haydon when they needed aid. In the latter's autobiography there is a bright account of a fortnight's visit paid by these two to Coleorton, Sir George's country-seat, which brings the interior life there vividly to the eye, though

it borrows something from the uncouscious
humor of the narrator, who always fills the
scene with himself in the leading part. One
pauses to note a characteristic sentence of
the incorrigible beggar in which he breaks
out with the indignant remark, " All my
friends were always advising me what to do
instead of advising the Government what to
do for me." Sir George, however, had other
friends, and most noteworthy of all, Wordsworth, of whom he first heard from Coleridge. Before meeting him, understanding
that the two friends wished to live in the
same neighborhood, he bought and presented
to Wordsworth the little property of Apple-
thwaite near Greta Hall, Coleridge's abode.
Wordsworth never used the ground for the
purpose for which it was given, but it remained in his possession. From this time,
1803, a close friendship grew up between
his family at Grasmere and the one at Coleorton, grounded upon common interests and
cemented with mutual exchanges of kindness and regard, so that it survived until
the death of Sir George and Lady Beaumont, herself an excellent woman, of whom
Crabb Robinson wrote, " She is a gentle-
woman of great sweetness and dignity, I

should think among the most interesting persons in the country."

Of the two poets Coleridge was at first more intimate with the Beaumonts. This was in 1803, the period of his illness, just previous to the voyage to Malta. The letters he wrote are very painful to read. The subject is usually the ego; and in reading the apologies of the writer for treating of this ever-present theme, and his observations on his own lack of vanity and the danger he is in of undervaluing his powers and works, one can scarcely fail to be struck by the identity in many respects of the egotism of the overweening and of the self-depreciating kinds. The aspects are different, but the weakness has the same root. In Coleridge it was, perhaps, no more than a question of the state of his stomach whether his assiduous interest in himself should result in intellectual pride or in self-abasement; but without giving too severe a touch, it is clear enough that his eye, when fixed on himself, was on the wrong object.

The letters to the Beaumonts are characterized by this complaining and absorbing egotism of the invalid, unfortified by patience, resolution, or even self-respect. The

ravages of disease in its physical aspects, the
laying bare of bodily conditions and symp-
toms of decay, would be in themselves intol-
erably disagreeable, but it is much worse to
be obliged to attend at the sick-bed of the
mind ; and in Coleridge's case the internal
weakness of the spirit excites the greatest
pity, and this feeling nearly passes involuntarily into disgust. The sensibility of his
nervous organization was acute. He speaks
of times when, as he was accusing himself
of insensibility through incapacity to feel, his
" whole frame has gone *crash*, as it were."
Under the excitement of his emotions, he
dissolves in weakness ; the spectacle is not
a pleasant one ; there is something almost
ignoble in such loss of self-control. When
Wordsworth recited to him, if one can fancy
such a thing, the entire thirteen books on
the growth of his own mind, in 1807, Coleridge composed a poem, not very coherent or
noble, though with personal pathos, in which
he says that when he rose from his seat, he
" found himself in prayer." It was apparently not an unusual termination to the access of emotion, and it occurred more than
once in his relations with the Beaumonts.
The mention of it, however, in his corre-

spondence with them, offends one, not in itself, but by the manner of it; indeed, the manner of his earlier letters is indescribable. Their sentiment is so tremulous and overwrought with fever that they resemble maundering; they are "sicklied o'er" with mental disease, and belong to the pathology of genius.

One long epistle, in which he devotes himself to an analysis of his mental condition at the time when he was what is now known as a Social Democrat, shows by an eminent example in what ways the minds of young men of enthusiasm, who have caught the contagion of new ideas, commonly act, and how their tongues are kept going. Coleridge and Southey were rampant young radicals for about ten months, and might many times have been justly thrown into jail for the use of unlawful language and seditiously fomenting the passions of the people. Coleridge ascribes the beginning of his ramblings from the true path of respectable politics partly to his intellectual isolation among his relatives and virtuous acquaintances generally, who thought that his "opinions were the drivel of a babe, but the guilt attached to them, — this was the

gray hair and rigid muscle of inveterate
depravity;" and partly, he declares, it was
due to the thirst for kindness planted in
himself, in that "*me*, who," he says, "from
my childhood have had no avarice, no ambition, whose very vanity in my vainest moments was nine tenths of it the desire and
delight and necessity of loving and of being
beloved," — needs which he found satisfied
in the welcome and company of "the Dem-
ocrats."   So he fell among evil companions.
On becoming an agitator upon the platform
he succumbed to the temptations of the
fluent speaker, gifted "with an ebullient
fancy, a flowing utterance, a light and dan-
cing heart, and a disposition to catch time
by the very rapidity of my own motion, and
to speak vehemently from mere verbal associations ; choosing sentences and sentiments
for the very reason which would have made
me recoil with a dying away of the heart
and unutterable horror from the actions expressed in such sentiments and sentences,
namely, because they were wild and original,
and vehement and fantastic."   Here is a
choice specimen of his eloquence, on the occasion of a supper by some Lord, to com-
memorate an Austrian victory: "This is a

true Lord's Supper in the communion of darkness! This is a Eucharist of Hell! a sacrament of misery! over each morsel and each drop of which the spirit of some murdered innocent cries aloud to God, This is my body! and this is my blood!" There is one sin against society, however, which he declined to commit, and he took great credit to himself for his obstinate refusal. He joined no party, club, or any of the radical societies, which he characterizes as "ascarides in the bowels of the state, subsisting on the weakness and diseasedness, and having for their final object the death of that state, whose life had been their birth and growth, and continued to be their sole nourishment." He remained outside of these entangling alliances, a free-lance speechifier, in the condition of mind of the willing martyr: "The very clank of the chains that were to be put about my limbs would not at that time have deterred me from a strong phrase or striking metaphor, although I had had no other inducement to the use of the same except the wantonness of luxuriant imgination, and my aversion to abstain from anything simply because it was dangerous." Such was Coleridge at twenty-four years, —

the age at which Emmett was executed; whose death called out this long letter of reminiscences concerning his own career as an agitator, and of reflections upon the impulses and justification of revolutionary orators, their tempations, errors, and illusions. He understood the fate of Emmett with greater clearness because of this little episode in his own life, and it is noticeable that he has the grace not to think that the young patriot's career bore too much resemblance to his own; but this confession of his foolishness in general, spread out somewhat magniloquently before the eyes of his aristocratic correspondent, is a lesson in human nature well worth a moment's attention from conservative and orderly people.

Coleridge's career — if a brief digression may be pardoned here — was only too much in keeping with the temperament of these letters to the Beaumonts. Wherever one comes upon it in the memoirs of the time, the story is the same. Soften it as we may, that career was one of those, too frequent among men of letters, that can never be told, so marred by disease and by moral feebleness, so full of shame and supineness and waste, that it must be kept out of sight.

During the years of his maturity he was a broken man, and knew himself to be such; from the time that, in becoming the victim of opium, he lost what little will-power was originally his, he felt that the spirit of imagination had left his house of life, and in its place was henceforward

> "Sense of past youth, and manhood come in vain,
> And genius given, and knowledge won in vain;"

and in this mood of pervading despondency he seems always in fancy to be haunting the grave of his dead self. This consciousness of his loss, though it had more of the stupor of despair than of the sharpness of penitence, lends some impressiveness to his story; but this pain was not searching enough to save him for himself, nor of a kind to make men oblivious of those violent contrasts in his life which offend our sense of rightness. It is a morally confusing spectacle to see genius professing the highest knowledge of the secret things of God, but itself wrecked; and it requires something more than the poet's sorrow at the withering of his wreath to reconcile such an antithesis.

Then, too, although Coleridge's poetic imagination undoubtedly was quenched at once, or gave out only brief and random flashes in his manhood, it may well be questioned whether the waste of his faculties was not due quite as much to mismanagement of the mind as to the palsying of his powers of effort, purpose, or orderly reduction of thought. He lived in the period of universal philosophers, and in his study of metaphysics and theology in Germany he must have fixed in his mind the habit of including the *omne scibile* in his system. This was the more easy for him, as he had in unusual proportion that false comprehensiveness which seizes on knowledge, not by all its relations as it stands in the body of science, but by some particular relation which it may seem to bear, truly or untruly, to some preconceived idea that has been taken as the organizing principle of the new scheme. It is because of their common participation in this method that poetry and philosophy, in the old sense, approach so much nearer each other than either does to science. It is plain to any one who reads the topics of Coleridge's discourses that his mind ranged through a vast circuit of knowledge habitually, but also that it touched the facts only at single points and superficially; in other words, he displays compass rather than grasp. In dealing with the mass of his learning, he showed no lack of systematizing power, though it may easily be believed that in conversation with chance visitors the fine filaments of logical connection escaped their sight. The trouble was in the original mode of elaborating the system — the old Greek way of philosophizing by subtle manipulation of analogies, convenient facts, half-understood harmonies of this with that, arbitrary constructions, with now and then a dead plunge into the unfathomable. To borrow Coleridge's own distinction, this procedure is to logic what fancy is to the imagination — a freak of the mind partly out of relation to the truth of things. It is the modern form of scholasticism.

Coleridge, however, whose speculative powers were thus employed, is believed to have been a great light to those who had eyes to see. What particular truth Maurice and others derived from him is, nevertheless, not evident. He shared the awakening power that idealists possess, generally in proportion to their consistency and the intensity of their personal conviction. Idealism, by the very fact that it is an enfranchisement from

sense, is a tonic to the mind; it quickens
the activity of thought and facilitates its
processes because it assumes the mastery of
the universe, and makes reality pliable to its
hand. This may or may not be lawful, but
it generates a feeling of command and of
liberty highly favorable to spiritual development. To some men impressionable on that
side of their nature Coleridge was the giver
of this freedom, and this has been the case
especially with members of the clergy who
are closely attached to theological dogma.
Such persons found in Coleridge's mind the
rare and curious coexistence of fixed dogma
with incessant speculation: he afforded the
sense of untrammeled investigation without
once disturbing the certainty of the pre-
judged cause. This phantom of liberalism
was a very quieting tutelar genius to some
educated men, who thus kept up a semblance
of thinking; but influence of this sort is
necessarily transitory. His Scriptural ren-
derings of philosophy give place to those of
other theologians, who rationalize on new
grounds of scientific knowledge instead of
German metaphysics, while the stimulation
that was furnished by his idealism may be
more simply and directly derived from less

involved and abstruse thinkers. His theology and metaphysics, in pursuit of which he wasted his powers, are already seen to be transient. On the other hand, his criticism has articulated the works of minor authors who have themselves written in a formal style, nor has its influence been harmed by its frequent over - refinement and fancifulness; and his poetry has remained untouched by time. It belongs to the period of his early enthusiasm, before he had become too dulled for the breath of inspiration to kindle him; and fortunately one can read nearly all the best of it without a thought of the dreary after - life of the poet, which has no vital interest to any one except as an illustration of prolonged failure due to many causes, but not less to a lack of mental than of moral self-government. He infiltrated a peculiar intellectual life into the clergy of his time, but in them it came to nothing more tangible and permanent than in himself. Will it be long before Carlyle's picture of the Seer at Highgate will be the only supplement to The Ancient Mariner, so far as the general knowledge of Coleridge is concerned, and all between nothing but the weariness of the opium-eater's hiding?

Perhaps the serenity of Wordsworth's home at Grasmere gains by the miserable contrast. Thither Coleridge came for invigoration; thither, when he finally separated from his wife, he brought or sent the children; and when he could not or would not retire to the hospitality and pleasant companionship of the household where he found the feminine sympathy which he had failed of in his own marriage, Wordsworth would set out to visit him with moral support and cheer. A different interest united Wordsworth and Sir George Beaumont; it was the love of nature. Landscape was the subject of their thoughts. Sir George painted it, Wordsworth poetized it; in the life of both it was a permanent resource to which they constantly resorted, and they liked to blend their work in this solvent — the pictures of the one becoming a text for the poems of the other, and *vice versa*. The interest Wordsworth felt in landscape gardening, in modifying wild nature, and his ideas regarding the methods and aims of the art, are brought out by the part he had in planning the grounds at Coleorton. Sir George rebuilt these, and, in laying out the winter garden in particular, he had frequent recourse to the taste of his friend; and as Wordsworth was that year occupying the old farmhouse on the estate, the business of thinking out and overseeing this work was at once diversion and restful employment amid his poetic labors. He wrote at great length on the subject to Lady Beaumont, and laid before her an elaborate plain full of ivy, holly, juniper, yews, open sunshine glades, flower-borders, an alley, a bower, a spray-fountain, a quarry, a distant spire, a pool with two gold-fish, a vine-clad old cottage, and other things which are artificial enough in the reading, but in reality seem remarkably well fitted to mingle the charm of cultivation with the wildness of the evergreens, and make a sheltering retreat where the life of nature would linger longest in autumn and revive earliest in the warm sun.

"Painters and poets," he wrote, "have had the credit of being reckoned the fathers of English gardening," and he felt thus in the line of succession in the art. It is most interesting to observe how he obtains suggestions from the poets, and makes their Pegasus plough his field. He was, of course, opposed to undue interference with nature

and the deformity it occasions, and also to
the ostentation of the wealth or station of
the owner. " It is a substitution of little
things for great when we would put a whole
country into a nobleman's livery," he says
with spirit, and, declaring that the laying
out of grounds is a liberal art not unlike
poetry and painting, he goes on to protest against the monopoly of nature by the
great ones of the earth, upon high æsthetic
grounds. " No liberal art," he says, "aims
merely at the gratification of an individual
or a class; the painter or poet is degraded
in proportion as he does so. . . . If this
be so when we are merely putting together
words or colors, how much more ought the
feeling to prevail when we are in the midst
of the realities of things. . . . What, then,
shall we say of many great mansions with
their unqualified expulsion of human crea-
tures from their neighborhood, happy or
not — houses which do what is fabled of
the upas tree — that they breathe out death
and desolation?" These strictures on the
aristocratic handling of land he continues
for some pages in an interesting advocacy
of æsthetic communism — still a suggestive
topic. This sense of the beauty and gran-

deur of nature as a universal boon, the desire to humanize the landscape without robbing it of its own essential character or of the minor charms of its native wildness, and a great delight in his own practical work of improving rubbish heaps, old walls, and broken ground into a winter retreat of sunshine and evergreens and red-berried vines, with nooks and views fit for a poet's walk, are the qualities that still give interest to those half dozen letters about planting a waste acre of land.   On the other hand, his genius, in which susceptibility to nature was so dominating a principle, seldom finds expression in the prose of his letters with nearly the same clearness and purity as in his poems.   There is one extract, however, which must be given, of a city scene from the country poet : —

" I left Coleridge at seven o'clock on Sunday morning and walked towards the city in a very thoughtful and melancholy state of mind. I had passed through Temple Bar and by St. Dunstan's, noticing nothing, and entirely occupied with my own thoughts, when, looking up, I saw before me the avenue of Fleet Street, silent, empty, and pure white, with a sprinkling of new-fallen snow, not a cart or a carriage to obstruct the view, no noise, only a few soundless and dusky foot-passengers here and there. You remember the elegant line of the curve of Ludgate Hill in which the avenue would terminate, and beyond, and towering above it, was the huge and majestic form of St. Paul's, solemnized by a thin veil of falling snow. I cannot say how much I was affected at this unthought-of sight in such a place, and what a blessing I felt there is in habits of exalted imagination. My sorrow was controlled, and my uneasiness of mind — not quieted and relieved altogether — seemed at once to receive the gift of an anchor of security."

This is not poetry, but it is from the same pen as the sonnet on Westminster Bridge.

Besides this taste for landscape, a special interest was taken by both friends in what poetry Wordsworth was composing from time to time. Wordsworth again expatiates on the " awful truth that there neither is, nor can be, any genuine enjoyment of poetry among·nineteen out of twenty of those persons who live, or wish to live, in the broad light of the world," that is, in society ; and again defines his aims, " to console the afflicted; to add sunshine to daylight, by making the happy happier; to teach the young and the gracious of every age to see, to think, and feel, and therefore become, more actively and securely virtuous," etc. Here, too, are the calm and patient confidence in his own immortality, a serene foreknowledge of how the matter would end, though there are some dark spots in his prevision, as when he says that "the people would love Peter Bell" if only the critics would let them. It appears, too, that these poets were discreet in their confidential criticism of each other, and by no means blind to faults. Wordsworth notices that in Southey's verse, notwithstanding picturesqueness and romance and a minor touch or two, "there is nothing that shows the hand of the great master;" and Coleridge, with all his adoration for Wordsworth, even when declaring that he regarded the tale of the ruined cottage in the Excursion as "the finest poem in our language, comparing it with any of the same or similar length," could yet put his finger on the very centre of weakness in Wordsworth. "I have sometimes fancied," he says, "that, having by the conjoint operation of his own experiences, feelings, and reason *himself* convinced *himself* of truths which the generality of people have either taken for granted from their infancy, or at least adopted in early life, he has attached all their own depth and weight to doctrines and words which come almost as truisms or commonplace to others."

Wordsworth's last words are a farewell; they illustrate how the love of nature and enjoyment of it, unlike most of youthful emotions, gain an increasing glow with years, and they express his faith and life in the most elementary terms: "I never had a higher relish for the beauties of nature than during this spring, nor enjoyed myself more. What manifold reason, my dear George, have you and I had to be thankful to Providence! Theologians may puzzle their heads about dogmas as they will; the religion of gratitude cannot mislead us. Of that we are sure, and gratitude is the handmaid to hope, and hope the harbinger of faith. I look abroad upon nature, I think of the best part of our species, I lean upon my friends, and I meditate upon the Scriptures, especially the Gospel of St. John; and my creed rises up of itself with the ease of an exhalation, yet a fabric of adamant. God bless you, my ever dear friend."

THREE MEN OF PIETY

I. BUNYAN.

THE word genius is often used to conceal a puzzle which the critic, through defects of analytic power or sympathetic insight, is unable to solve ; but perhaps this short and easy method was never more feebly resorted to than when a writer, with a strong prejudice in favor of sweetness and light, described Bunyan as a " Philistine of genius." In this designation there is much darkness and some acerbity. The wonderful thing about this man was not so much his gifts as the strange combination of them. There must be, of course, something extraordinary in any common man who becomes a leader in the higher life of the race. The history of the Church, however, is starred with the names of the ignorant and the humble who, since the fishermen were called from their nets by Galilee, have been chosen to be shepherds of the flock and evangelists of the faith. Bunyan was visited with the experience of Protestant Christendom, of which the successive terms are an outraged conscience, an offended God, and a miraculous pardon, and when he came to his peace he spread the glad news, acceptably to the pious, and convincingly to the impenitent; but tens of thousands in Christian lands have passed through that same strait gate, and hundreds of them have discovered that they possessed the gift of tongues. Had Bunyan done no more his sermons would have turned to yellow dust long ago, and his memory would be treasured only by a sect, for, eloquent as he was, he was not one of the missionaries who are world-famous. He wrote a book; and it turned out that this book of an uneducated man was a great literary classic. Had he written an epic it would have seemed less marvelous, because there is a popular superstition that nature makes poets, but in prose does not enter into competition with the common school. Bunyan wrote verses, it is true, and the man who set the delectable mountains on the rim of earth had the magical sight; but just as surely his doggerel shows that he had not the singing voice. He was a master of prose, and wrote a book that neighbors the Bible in our religious homes.

Two things are, of course, indispensable to a boy of genius, — imagination and the gift of expression. Now Bunyan was fond of representing himself as very wicked in youth; and so he was, from his own point of view. The worst he can say for himself is, that he lied and swore, without malice or injury to others, but because he had a talent for tales and oaths. It is not trifling to remark that his powers of invention and forcible Saxon speech appear to have found their first channel in this sort of mental activity. The possible openings for the development of genius in the tinker's cottage at Bedford were few. It is plain that the mind of the young man was one of intense life, and, in the lack of guidance and knowledge, wandered at random or turned to feed upon itself. The only intellectual or moral ideas that came to him were conveyed from the Bible, mostly through the medium of the parish church in the years of the Puritan ascendency. The commonplace that the Bible affords a good education, especially on the imaginative and moral sides, is true, and the theology that attaches to it has developed strong intellects; it was, in the end, the total book-culture of Bunyan, — all that he knew of that vast and various world. But in the primary classes it is not a simple text-book of life, especially for a boy of genius who is all sense, all spirit. Bunyan in after years did not regret his first lessons; he preached that children should be taught the terrors of the law. Certainly his own mind laid hold of the easily apprehended images of threatened vengeance, and was filled with vague alarm and driven to a torturing scrutiny of his own spirit. The experience of conversion repeats in the individual the religious history of the race in the same order in which it is developed in the evolution of Biblical thought itself, and Bunyan's case was not substantially different from that of others, Puritan or Catholic, to whom there is no Calvary without a Sinai. The peculiarity lay in the soil into which this fiery seed was sown. His imagination ceased its childish fabling and became visionary; he saw, as the eye sometimes will, his mind-pictures, and this the more readily because his uneducated mind was accustomed to move through concrete ideas, and hence would be characterized by a high visualizing power. That this was a marked trait of his mental habit is shown by the fact that all his stories about himself are localized in a distinctly remembered place.

At this stage his mind approached the danger-line of religious madness: his descriptions of his moods, of his despairs, and of his struggles with fancies, whose importance to his intellectual life arose from the fewness of his ideas and the limited field of their play, show that he had no power over his thoughts, that he had not learned to use his will in thinking. This objectivity of his religious experience and his powerlessness before it, which have been recorded of other intense lives likewise, gave him a strong sense of the reality of spiritual things; and when he at last had laid his doubts and come into the calm, he kept this conviction to such a degree that earthly matters, even when religion was largely interested in politics, seemed of no consequence: this world was the dream, and the next world the truth. To our days the account of this conversion seems to indicate a lack of sanity, a spirit touched with the fever that ends in fanaticism; but we may be sure that to his hearers there was nothing incredible in it, nothing that could not be paralleled out of what they had known in themselves or heard from their neighbors. So, early in life, the plot of his career was brought to its crisis. In this faith in the reality of eternal things his mind reached its growth, and afterward knew no change.

But with this sure hold on the spirit and its high concerns there went a perfect realism. Bunyan was the opposite of a mystic. His common sense in his sermons of advice is extraordinarily close-packed and hard, and exhibits acute observation of the ways of human nature in practical life. He wrote once what was almost a novel, a history of one Mr. Badman, which is probably truer to contemporary life than the adventures of Jonathan Wild in the next century. If he did not weaken his eyesight over books, he sharpened it on men and women. All his volumes abound with anecdotes and incidents which he had evidently seen in the town streets or by the roadside, and with phrases and proverbial sayings close to the soil. Not the least agreeable of the signs of this realism, this sight for the bare fact in sense alone, are those descriptions of the country, of the birds, and flowers, and fields, and the simple cheerfulness of them to the country-born boy, which strew his pages from cover to cover. So, when he came to write his great book, he united in a perfectly natural way, and without forethought, the reality of a journey on earth with that of the search for heaven. The success with which, in a literary work, truth is fused with fact, is a measure of genius. It is, perhaps, more striking in this case because the work is an allegory, which is usually so drearily pale a kind of composition. The characters and action of the Pilgrim's Progress, on the contrary, are a transcript of life, so vivid that it cannot wear out. It is not more realistic, however, than other portions of Bunyan's voluminous writings, in which one may get an idea of English provincial character of high historical value and human interest. How close, how truthful to his surroundings he was as a literary workman, is brought home with great force, though perhaps unconsciously, by the view which his biography gives of Bedford things and people.

From it one may reconstruct the religious state of the poor people of the Lincoln diocese in Bunyan's time, and bring very near the look of the lowly life which was the original soil of English dissent and the field

of the tinker - preacher's labors. In reading terse extracts from the old documents —
" short and simple annals of the poor," truly
— of prayers in the barn and fines in the
court - house, of levies on workmen's tools
and old women's chattels, of these families
of " the meanest sort," as the Bishop's sched-
ule calls them, whose petty share of poverty
was confiscated for the security of a Stuart
throne and an Anglican prayer - book, — in
reading of these things, a chapter of the history of the English people comes out which
has been too closely written over with the
wit and frolic of Charles's court ; and the
query as to what became of the Commonwealth when Cromwell died does not seem so
wholly unanswerable as the silence of standard history on the point would indicate.

After all, one is almost inclined to say
that no man ever owed more than Bunyan to
his limitations. Within his bounds, he used
all his spiritual and earthly experience, and,
aided by a native gift of imagination and of
fluency in the people's speech, blended them,
and poured the full fountain of his life
through his books.   Had his youth included
other powerful elements of emotion and
knowledge besides his conversion, had theol-

ogy, or learning, or wider duties removed him somewhat more from the life of his neighbors and friends and the folk of the diocese, of which he was jestingly called the "bishop," he might have found so complete self-expression a more difficult task. As it was, he told all he had to tell, — told the highest truth in the commonest words and made it current. It is curious to observe that he exhibits no consciousness that he is writing a great work; he speaks of a rush of thought and fancy, and an attractiveness in the subject, but he does not seem to think that he is doing more than adding another to the two-score publications he has already sent out. It is noticeable, too, that he did not meditate upon it for years beforehand, nor spend more than a few months in its composition. Some passages were added at a later time, but as a whole it was a spontaneous and rapid composition. The reason is that he was ripe for it. Without knowing it, he had been working up to this crowning book, both in thought, treatment, and style, through many years of sincere and straightforward, face-to-face conversation with men and women whom he was endeavoring to guide in the way which he had traveled. Pilgrim's Progress has been called the last book that was written without the fear of the reviewer; it is of more consequence that it is one of the few works that have been composed without ambition.

Bunyan's memory is singularly agreeable. Personally he was free from the defects of assumption, dogmatism, and spiritual pride, which entered largely into the religious character of his epoch, and his sensitive conscience seems to have kept him humble after he had won a name. The two great elements of his work — the homely quality and the Christian quality — were deep-seated in his nature, and give him charm. In an age of sectaries he was not a narrow bigot, and did not stickle for meaningless things; and in a time of political strife, growing out of religious differences, and though himself a sufferer by twelve years' imprisonment in early manhood, he did not confuse heaven with any fantastic monarchy or commonwealth of Christ in London, nor show any rancor or revengeful spirit as a subject. It is worth remembering that out of Puritanism, which is regarded as a narrow creed and life, came the only book since the Reformation which has been acceptable to the whole of Christendom, and is still regarded as the substantial truth of the Christian life in all the churches that preach it under any creed of orthodoxy. The life of the man who could evolve such a story must have been very simply typical of the Christian life itself. "A Philistine of genius" — is there no light nor sweetness in this?

II. COWPER.

The career of Cowper, as all the world knows, was one to fill the pessimist with perennial gladness; and, in fact, if it were possible to look at the natural order of things only as Cowper was affected thereby, it might seem that nothing short of malignity in the overruling powers could account for the fiat that gave up so pure, simple, and cordial a nature to be the prey of the seven devils, and rendered so many delightful traits of character futile to achieve the happiness of their unfortunate possessor. In his letters, flowing on in the old, sweet, fresh English, one perceives the rare literary faculty, the shy humor, the discrimination, the sound sense, all the many graces of style and many virtues of intrinsic worth, that have long been familiar to scholars; and, more than that, one gladly recognizes again the companionable, soft-hearted, pathetic man whose pastimes, whether in gardening, or poetry, or caring for his pets, were a refuge from the most poignant anguish ; who played only to escape his terror, and at last failed even in that. The piety of Cowper's life, however, although it contributes to his poetic attractiveness, is only a small part of what must be dealt with by the observer of that life as it appears in his familiar letters. These, as a body, it is needless to say, hold a place from which they are not likely to be dislodged. Nevertheless, letters at the best are not a high form of literature; even when, as in the present case, their workmanship entitles them to rank as classics, their interest must finally reside in their being unconscious autobiography rather than in their artistic perfection. Hence, instead of regarding this correspondence as an object of literary *virtu*, it may be well for once to consider it with a more direct reference to the sober facts it chronicles and the spirit it reveals.

Few persons experienced in the world would be likely to hold up the routine of Cowper's days as worthy of imitation. So

far as earthly matters were involved, it was
a life of very small things; its mundane interests were few and trivial, and sprang for
the most part out of pursuits that belong
usually either to the domain of childhood or
of invalidism. This is not said disparag-
ingly, but with due regard to the fact that
for the larger part of his career Cowper's
condition was such that his attention had to
be distracted and his mind amused, as is the
case with children or invalids. In his later
years the composition of verses became one
mode of such diversion, and was undertaken
practically as a sanitary measure; and thus
his larger interests, involving conceptions of
the eternal world and sympathy with his fellow-men, were extended to his hours of recreation. These larger interests, as they
must be called, were from the first peculiar.
When he was not attending to his hares or
his vegetables, or versifying, or taking rural
walks, he was engaged in devotional exercises of one kind or another. In 1766, for
example, every day the time from breakfast
until eleven o'clock was spent in reading the
Bible or sermons, or in religious conversation; the hour from eleven to twelve was
passed in church at service; in the course of

the afternoon there was a second period of religious conversation or hymn-singing; at night there was commonly another sermon and more psalms, and after that family prayers. In other words, it appears that Cowper's life, at that time at least (and it is a fair sample of the whole), consisted of an almost monastic religious routine, relieved by the diversion of country pursuits on a small scale, and, later, of literary pursuits in addition. At present, as has been said, few qualified judges would consider this a life of high order, either in the way of wisdom or utility; but in Cowper's case, the peculiarity of his mental condition and the charm of his nature, revealed at its happy moments in pleasant letters, blind the reader to the monotony and vapidity of this existence, for such were its characteristics, except in so far as the healing influences of natural scenes, to which Cowper was very sensitive, and the kindness of his household friends, gave it variety and substance.

Now, it is a very striking fact that while Cowper spent the larger part of his time in religious reading and conversation, and besides meditated in private on the same themes, his letters do not show in any degree

that insight into spiritual things which would
naturally be looked for from real genius
occupied with such subjects. Spirituality
should have been his trait if religion was
his life, but, in fact, these letters are in this
regard barren. The anomalous nature of
his poetic life — the fact that he used his
powers, not to express his deepest emotions,
but to escape from them — may be pleaded
in extenuation of what seems at first a surprising defect; but a more likely explanation lies in another direction. It was sermons that he read, theology that he talked
about, a theory of grace and salvation that
he meditated upon in secret; his religion
occupied his thoughts rather than his acts,
touched his future rather than his present,
— in a word, it was a system rather than a
life, the source of doubt instead of inspiration. To put it in the simplest form, he
derived his light, not from his own inner experience, but from the creed. In his case
the light was the darkness of insanity; but
his own conviction in the matter is shown
in his characterization of Beattie, — "a man
whose faculties have now and then a glimpse
from Heaven upon them, a man not indeed
in possession of much evangelical light, but

faithful to what he has, and never neglecting an opportunity to use it." A poet who identifies " evangelical light " with " the vision and the faculty divine " may write The Castaway, but one is not likely to find in his works those intimate revelations of truth that flash in convincing beauty from the lines of the true spiritualists, such as Wordsworth, Shelley, or Emerson. Cowper's misfortune, both as a man and a poet, was this substitution of dogma for instinct, which, operating in so sensitive and feeble a nature, made religion, which was his vital interest, not a life but a disease, and gave to the activities of his higher powers the character of mania. It is misleading, therefore, to think of these letters as the fruit of a deeply religious mind; they are the record of the efforts of a creed-believing mind to get rid of itself, and their virtues — their amiability, their delight in small adventures, their interest in literature and humanity — exist not in consequence of but in spite of the religious bent of their author.

Cowper was deficient, too, æsthetically as well as spiritually, and the character of his limitations was much the same in both respects. His sense of beauty was practically confined to landscape and small animals. The cramping influences amid which he lived are well indicated by his remarks upon a clergyman who, it should be said, richly deserved censure : —

" He seems, together with others of our acquaintance, to have suffered considerably in his spiritual character by his attachment to music. The lawfulness of it, when used with moderation, and in its proper place, is unquestionable; but I believe that wine itself, though a man be guilty of habitual intoxication, does not more debauch and befool the natural understanding than music — always music, music in season and out of season — weakens and destroys the spiritual discernment. If it is not used with an unfeigned reference to the worship of God, and with a design to assist the soul in the performance of it, which cannot be the case when it is the only occupation, it degenerates into a sensual delight, and becomes a most powerful advocate for the admission of other pleasures, grosser, perhaps, in degree, but in their kind the same."

Whatever truth there may be in this estimate of the influence of music, the limitation of its use to church choirs and organs is an expression of Puritan iconoclasm which acquaints the reader at once with Cowper's provincialism. The passage is English to the core, and not only does it suggest the æsthetic deficiencies of the poet and his life, but it also brings up once more the characteristic English picture of the family singing psalms and reading sermons, year in, year out, with which the letters begin. This correspondence has made that group of interest to the world; but in answer to the question, What was its life and its spirit, can one help feeling that trivial, not to say belittling, occupations, and a narrowing theology, were principal elements? Cowper's work, in the main, has only the sluggish vitality of this life; in his letters more than in his verses, speaking generally, there is literary grace and personal charm; but in both they seem a sort of salvage. A vision of quiet green fields, inhabited by respectable gentlefolk who led an existence of humble routine in a neighborly way, made up Cowper's world; he lived in it overshadowed by the ever present fear of damnation, and at last, sunk in despair, he died in it. Out of such a world no great poet either of the soul or of nature could come.

Cowper's virtue was in his simplicity and genuineness, rare qualities then; his good fortune was in never belonging to the literary set or bowing to the town taste; hence in a time the most barren in English literature, he gave us a half dozen fine poems that stand far beyond all contemporary rivalry, and some private letters of the best style and temper. When, however, the question comes as to the intrinsic value of these letters, it must be confessed that though they please the taste they do not interest the mind except in a curious and diverting way. They are less the letters of a poet than of a village original, a sort of schoolmaster or clergyman *manqué*, of sound sense, tender heart, and humane perception, but the creature of a narrow sphere.

III. CHANNING.

Channing was the chief ornament of the American pulpit in his day. Like nearly all men illustrious in the religious life, he has won a kindlier and wider regard by his character than by his opinions, because the moods of devotion are simple and are universal in human nature, while opinion in theology is more variable and eccentric, and in some degree more accidental, than in any other branch of speculation. The deepest interest of his life lies not so much in the fruit of his genius as in the light of his spirit. Indeed, this acknowledgment is wrapped up in the indiscriminate eulogy by which his admirers have injured his fame, for they have presented him as a saint rather than as a thinker, as an example of ideal living rather than as a finder of truth. To put a man in the catalogue of saints is merely to write his epitaph; his life is the main thing, and Channing, although his biography records no great deeds in the world and no great crises of inner experience, is not alone in being far more interesting in his humanity than in his canonization. A refined and sensitive childhood, shadowed in some partially explained way, so that he never remembered it as a period of joyfulness, was followed by a spirited and dreaming youth, caught by the fervors of French revolutionary ideas and exalted by its own noble motives. In those early years, as well as in his late maturity, he experienced, on the beach at Newport and under the willows at Cambridge, moments of insight and impulse which stood out ever after in his memory as new births of the spirit prophetic of the future. His career was especially determined, however, by the twenty-one months which he passed at Richmond as a private tutor, immediately after leaving college. There, in loneliness and poverty, in stoical disregard of health and courting privation, in Christian conscientiousness of motive, led on by glowing reveries in which visionary objects seemed realities within reach, he devoted himself in written words to the service of mankind by the instrumentalities of religion. It is painful to read the narrative of this intense personal life in the years most susceptible to enthusiasm for remote and ideal ends; there can be no wonder that after such experience he returned home with the seal of the religious life set upon his soul, and with a body inexorably condemned to life-long disease. He entered upon his ministry in the field where he could best do good and find peace in doing it; morally the child of the New England religious spirit, and intellectually the disciple of those ideas of the nature of humanity and the right course of its development which the French Revolution had disseminated. Throughout his life he was governed mainly by a deep sense of the dignity of manhood, under whatever form, and by an abiding conviction of the aid which Christianity gives to the imagination and heart in obeying the rule of love and obtaining permanent peace of mind.

The most acute criticism ever passed upon Channing's character was by that unnamed critic who said, " He was kept from the highest goodness by his love of rectitude." The love of rectitude was his predominant trait; he was enslaved by it. He exacted more of himself, however, than of others. Right he must be, at all hazards, in motive, opinion, and action. It is melancholy to read page after page of his self-examination, so minute, intricate, and painful, so frequent and long continued. It almost awakens a doubt of the value of noble character to find it so unsure of itself, to see its possessor so absorbed in hunting his own shadow within the innermost retreats of thought and feeling. Channing seems to have preached more sermons to himself than to the world. His love of rectitude led him to this excessive conscientiousness, but it brought him great good in other directions. It gave him a respect for the opinions of other men as

catholic as it was humble. He did not
practice toleration toward them, for that expression implied to his mind a misplaced
self-confidence; but he practiced charity, as
toward men who felt equally with himself
the binding force of the obligation to be
right, and who had an equal chance of finding truth. His conviction of the universality of this obligation and his perception
that it necessitates the independent exercise
of individual powers encouraged in him a
remarkable admiration for individuality, for
the unhampered exercise of thought and un-
questioned obedience to motive in which the
richness of individual life consists.

His second great quality, as pervasive and
controlling as his desire to be right, was
sensibility. It was revealed in the sympathies and affections of private life, which
are known to the world only by the report
of friends; but it may be seen with equal
clearness in the intensity of his delight in
nature, and in the ardent feeling by which
he realized ideal ends and gave them a living presence in his own life as objects of
continuous effort. His sensitiveness to natural beauty was so keen that in moments of
physical weakness it caused pain. "There

are times," he wrote, " when I have been so feeble that a glance at the natural landscape, or even the sight of a beautiful flower, gave me a bodily pain from which I shrank." As life drew on to its end, the indestructible loveliness of nature became to him a source of joy and peace ever more prized. "The world grows younger with age!" he exclaimed more than once. In emotional susceptibility to ideas he resembled Shelley, and probably it was this likeness of feeling which led him to call Shelley, in ministerial language, but with extraordinary charity for that age, "a seraph gone astray." He retained through life the intellectual sympathies of his youth, and in his last days still had an inclination toward community of property as the solution of the social problem; like Wordsworth and Southey he recoiled from the excesses of the French, but he never gave up the tricolor for the white cockade. In his generation nearly all men were hopeful of the accomplishment of beneficent reforms; but Channing was filled with an enthusiasm of hope which was almost the fervor of conviction. He was without that practical enthusiasm which is aroused by the presence of great deeds immediately to be done; the objects for which he worked were far in the distance, scarcely discernible except from the mount of vision; but he was possessed by the enthusiasm which is kindled by the heat of thought and is wrapped in its own solitary flames, and he lived under the bright zenith of that mood of which Carlyle has shown the dark nadir and Teufelsdröch standing in its shadow gazing out over the sleeping city. These three principles — rectitude, sensibility, enthusiasm — were elemental in Channing's nature; and because they are moral, and not intellectual, he lived a spiritual rather than a mental life; he gained in depth rather than in breadth, and worked out his development by contemplation and prayer rather than by thought and act.

It appears strange, at first, that a man with these endowments should have been so conservative in opinion, and so little inclined to force upon the world what advanced opinions he did hold. A lover of truth unwilling to make proselytes, an enthusiast unwilling to act, seems an anomaly; but such was Channing's position. One cause of his aversion to pushing Unitarianism to its conclusion is found in the history

of his own conversion and in the character
of his attachment to the new faith; he was
a revolter of the heart; he was liberalized
by his feelings. " My inquiries," he said,
" grew out of the shock given to my moral
nature by the popular system of faith."
He was moved by sentiment in his rejec-
tion of Calvinism, and he was kept by
sentiment from giving up the theory of the
mysterious character and mission of Christ.
The strength of his feelings operated to
render him conservative, and the low estimate he apparently placed upon logical
processes contributed to the same end. " It
is a good plan," he wrote, " ever and anon
to make a clean sweep of that to which we
have arrived by logical thought, and take a
new view; for the mind needs the baptism
of wonder and hope to keep it vigorous and
healthy for intuition." Either this distrust
of the understanding working by logical
processes, or else a native inaptitude for
theological reasoning, prevented him from
following out his principles to their conclusion. If he had framed a system, he would
have held his views with greater certainty;
as it was, he not only allowed the greatest
liberty to individual opinion, but he dis-

trusted himself. " You young thinkers," he said, " have the advantage of us in coming without superstitious preoccupation to the words of Scripture, and are more likely to get the obvious meaning. *We* shall walk in shadows to our graves." The strength of in-bred sentiment could not be overpowered by such feeble intellectual conviction. He was a moral, not an intellectual, reformer; his work was not the destruction of a theology, but the spread of charity. He felt more than he rea-soned, and hence his rationalism was bounded, not by the unknown, but by the mystical. He was satisfied with this, and does not seem to have wished to make a definite statement of his beliefs. The whole matter is summed up by Miss Peabody when she says, " The Christianity which Dr. Channing believed . . . was a spirit, not a form of thought." A spirit of devotion toward the divine, a spirit of love toward the human, Channing preached to the world and illustrated by his life ; but a new form of thought which shows the intellectual advance that alone is fatal to conservatism, — this was no part of his gift to men.

In the antislavery cause his conservatism appears in a less pleasing light. Here he exhibited the scholar's reluctance to initiate reform, the scholar's perplexity before the practical barriers in the way of action. He was displeased by the rude voices about him, and frightened by the violence of determination which the reformers displayed. He looked to find the peace of the pulpit in the arena, and was bewildered by the alarms of the active strife. He did not choose his side until the last moment, and even then he delayed until he called down the just rebuke of May and the just defense that reformer made for his comrades: " The children of Abraham held their peace until at last the very stones have cried out, and you must expect them to cry out like the stones." Then, indeed, Channing showed that he was a Falkland on Cromwell's side, not acting without a doubt, but taking his place, nevertheless, openly and manfully beside the friend whom he had left alone too long. Yet he never lost, even in that stirring cause, the timidity of culture. He was of the generation of those cultivated men who earned for Boston the reputation for intellectual preëminence; but the political future of the country did not belong to him nor to his companions; it belonged to Garrison and Lincoln. Here it is that Father Taylor's keen criticism strikes home: " What a beautiful being Dr. Channing is! If he only had had any education!" Channing's education had been of the lamp, and not of the sword; it seemed to Father Taylor pitifully narrow and palsy-stricken beside his own experience of the world's misery. Channing's life affords one more illustration of the difficulty the cultivated man finds in understanding and forwarding reform in its beginning; but he deserves the credit of having rid himself of the prejudices and influences that marked the society in which he moved, to a greater degree, perhaps, than any other of his circle.

The value of Channing's work in religion and in reform will be differently rated by men, for his service was of a kind which is too apt to be forgotten. The intrinsic worth of his writings remains to be tested by time; but their historic worth, as a means of liberalizing the New England of his day, was great and memorable. He gave his right hand to Emerson and his left hand to Parker; and, although he could not accompany them on the way, he bade them Godspeed. It was, perhaps, mainly through his influence that they found the field prepared for them and the harvest ready, although he would not put his sickle in. It was largely due to him, also, that Boston became the philanthropic centre of the country. During his lifetime he won a remarkable respect and admiration. An exaggerated estimate of his eloquence, powers, and influence will continue to be held so long as any remain alive who heard his voice and remember its accents; in later times a truer judgment may be reached. Personally he was amiable, kindly, and courteous, notwithstanding the distance at which he seems to have kept all men. Dr. Walker said that conversation was always constrained in his study. In his nephew's narrative, it is said that the interview with him was " solemn as the visit to the shrine of an oracle." He himself told Miss Peabody after their friendship had lasted several years, that she had " the awe of the preacher " upon her. Finally, we read that no man ever freely laid his hand upon Channing's shoulder; and we wonder whether he ever remembered that St. John had " *handled* the Word made flesh." This self-seclusion, this isolation of sanctity, as it were, did not proceed from any value he set upon himself above his fellows; it was the natural failing of a man who lived much within himself, and who always meditated the loftiest of unworldly themes. He was a faithful and well-beloved friend; and if in this, as in other directions, he "failed of the highest goodness," there are few in the same walk of life who attain to equal sincerity, charity, and purity, or equal serviceableness to the world.

DARWIN'S LIFE.

THERE is nothing more useful to observe in the life of Darwin than its simplicity. He was the man of science as Marlborough was the soldier, and he was only that. From boyhood he refused all other ways of life and knowledge as by instinct, and in his maturity the ill health which ends the career of ordinary men only confirmed him in his own; he was always the collector, the investigator, or the theorizer. A second quality, which is general enough to be constantly attracting attention, is the thoroughly English character of his life. The stock from which he sprang was rich in old English qualities of vigor, sense, and originality; the house in which he was reared offers an excellent type of English family life, and was as good a place to be born in as could be desired for any son; his father's strong character, the influences of his older relatives, the ordinary schools he attended, the smallest incidents of his childhood, even the jokes of his play-fellows, belong to the moral climate of the old country ; and it does not need the grouse-shooting, the Cambridge undergraduate suppers, and the proposition that he should choose the Church for a profession to tell us where we are. Indeed, Darwin in his youth, spirited, cordial, and overflowing with health, in his early surroundings of English strength and kindness, was quite as attractive as in his quieter, and in some respects narrower, working life.

He certainly won upon the men whom he met at the outset of his career. "Looking back," he says, "I infer that there must have been something in me a little superior to the common run of youths : otherwise the above-mentioned men, so much older than me and higher in academical position, would never have allowed me to associate with them. Certainly I was not aware of any such superiority; and I remember one of my sporting friends, Turner, who saw me at work with my beetles, saying that I should some day be a Fellow of the Royal Society, and the notion seemed to me preposterous." Of these men Henslow was the most attached to him and interested in his success. He had not done much more than work at "his beetles," but his scientific taste was already the ruling genius of his life. It is surprising to see how completely he remained untouched by the ordinary influences of a university training; he thought in later years that his scholastic education had been a waste of time, and he seems justified when one perceives how little good he got from it. His was a mind that belonged to himself, self-fed, almost self-made; he lived his own life, and not another's, from the start; though his taste for collecting was hereditary, the persistence with which he gave himself up to following it, the completeness of his surrender to his one predominant talent, was his own. He was, nevertheless, better furnished with intellectual power than he appears to have believed. "From my earliest youth," he writes, "I have had the strongest desire to understand or explain whatever I observed, that is, to group all facts under some general laws." It is true that he started from some specific facts, had a definite, tangible problem to solve; but he felt the necessity to solve it. He differed from the collector in this, that his curiosity was not exhausted in gathering materials, but he must also order his materials; or to put it exactly, must organize his knowledge. This shows the great vitality of his reasoning faculty, which within its special range was really precocious. The native strength of his mind in this direction is also illustrated by the great pleasure he derived from reading Paley's Evidences. "The logic of this book," he declares, "and, as I may add, of his Natural Theology, gave me as much delight as did Euclid. The careful study of these works, without attempting to learn any part by rote, was the only part of the academical course which, as I then felt and as I still believe, was of the least use to me in the education of my mind. I did not at that time trouble myself about Paley's premises; and taking these in trust, I was charmed and convinced by the long line of argumentation." He acknowledges his inability in later life to follow trains of abstract reasoning, such as make the matter of metaphysics; but he was quite aware of his aptitude for inductive reasoning, and does not overestimate its influence in the composition of his great work. "Some of my critics have said, 'Oh, he is a good observer, but he has no power of reasoning!' I do not think that this can be true, for the Origin of Species is one long argument from the beginning to the end, and it has convinced not a few able men." His taste for collecting was a *sine qua non*, but it was this power of reasoning, however limited in range, that made him great; and it is as clearly to be seen in operation in his formative years as was the passion for collecting which was to feed it with material to work upon. His vivacity and energy no doubt counted much in winning for him the friendship of elder men, and he possessed that indefinable but potent quality of personal attractiveness; but Henslow in the beginning, as Lyell later, must have seen in him that happy conjunction of tastes and faculties which made his genius for science, or at least they must have perceived the promise of it.

All the circumstances of his life seem to have conspired to favor this special endowment. The very fact that the classics did nothing for him helped him: he was relieved from the confusion caused by complex and disturbing elements in a varied education; he had no difficulty in making his choice; he was not afterward drawn aside by the existence of other unsatisfied tastes, artificially cultivated; he had no ambition for that roundness of development which is a fetich of modern times; he did not fritter away his time and energy in directions in which he could not excel. It is not meant to hold up his luck in this respect as exemplary good fortune, but only to-emphasize the way in which it told on his success. He was not less happy in the exterior circumstances of his life, and in those things which come by a kind of hazard. His appointment to the Beagle was a Napoleonic opportunity, and in looking back he realized its value to the full: " The voyage of the Beagle has been by far the most important event in my life, and has determined my whole career; yet it depended on so small a circumstance as my uncle offering to drive me thirty miles to Shrewsbury, which few uncles would have done, and on such a trifle as the shape of my nose." But one ought not to exaggerate the element of chance; and though Captain Fitz-roy had continued to disapprove of Darwin's nose, and his uncle had not interfered to overcome the elder Darwin's objection to the voyage on the score that it would be an unbecoming adventure for a prospective clergyman, and on

other equally good or better grounds, yet we
might have had our great naturalist. The
voyage of the Beagle, nevertheless, was the
turning-point of Darwin's life. He obtained
in the course of it the first real training of
his mind; it brought before him several departments of science in such a way that he
approached them with active and original
thoughts, and was constantly forced into an
inquiring and bold attitude toward the novel
material he found; it gave him five years
alone with science, and free from any near
master to whom he might have formed the
habit of deferring. Huxley does not over-
state the material advantages that this training brought with it: " In Physical Geogra-
phy, in Geology proper, in Geographical
Distribution, and in Palæontology, he had
acquired an extensive practical training during the voyage of the Beagle. He knew of
his own knowledge the way in which the
raw materials of these branches of science
are acquired, and was therefore a most competent judge of the speculative strain they
would bear. That which he needed, after
his return to England, was a corresponding
acquaintance with Anatomy and development, and their relations to Taxonomy, and

he acquired this by his Cirripede work." It is to be noticed that during his voyage in the Beagle he became convinced of the "wonderful superiority of Lyell's manner of treating geology" over every other author's. This is an illustration, like that drawn from Paley, of the character of his mind as primarily a reasoning mind; for what he recognized in Lyell was a method. It was on this voyage, too, that he became ambitious; he began to believe that he might add to the stock of human knowledge, and the stimulation of the welcome his success was meeting in England was evidently keenly felt. He put his whole heart into the work, and few passages are more stirring than those which describe his zeal in his first really scientific enthusiasm, after he had given up his gun as of less use than his eye, and had found sport, even with his fond love of it, an inferior pleasure to the pursuit of knowledge; then, alone in the Andes and the Southern Ocean, he came to his majority.

Mr. Huxley, in the passage cited, has noted the need Darwin had for further training, particularly as a naturalist. He obtained this by his work on the Cirripedes,

an eight years' labor. This concluded his
education. Of the value of it merely as
training and to himself, Sir Joseph Hooker
says : " Your father recognized three stages
in his career as a biologist : the mere collector at Cambridge ; the collector and observer in the Beagle, and for some years
afterwards ; and the trained naturalist after,
and only after, the Cirripede work. That
he was a thinker all along is true enough."
Huxley says that Darwin never did a wiser
thing than when he devoted himself to these
years of patient toil. Darwin himself does
not indicate that he purposely chose to do
this monograph in order to educate himself,
and he doubts whether it was worth the
time. He seems to have been gradually
drawn into it, and to have finished it because he had gone so far. When he had
done with it, at any rate, if not before, he
was a thoroughly furnished man for such investigation as was to be his title to lasting
fame. He had come to be thus equipped
by the mere course of his life ; by beetles
at Cambridge, and the Beagle, and the Cirripedes. Yet if he had planned his education from the start for the express purpose
of dealing in the most masterly way with

the mass of diversified details out of which the Origin of Species and the other derivative coördinate works grew, it is hard to see in what way his course could have been improved. The ill-health which seized him so soon was almost a blessing in disguise, since it isolated him from the distractions of modern London, made him value his life and his time, and possibly, by the economy of his strength which it necessitated, aided as much as it hindered him.

One need not follow him through the composition of his books, or even through the elaboration of the theory of natural selection, during the many years that it was growing in his laboratory of notes. For him the formulating of that theory was inevitable: it seems, as one observes him, natural enough to have been foretold of him; but it followed, not from his position, which another man might have occupied, but from his genius. The qualities of mind which it required were not many, and one understands readily why it is so commonly said that all is explained by his power of observation and its vast range; but it did require one high faculty of the mind, and a rare one, which Darwin had preëminently among the men of his time, — the faculty, namely, of discerning the lines of inquiry in a mass of as yet unrelated facts. He somewhere says that he had found it harder, perhaps, to put the question than it was to reach the answer. This power is the great economizer of mental energy, in any branch of investigation; it is, to the man who has it, equivalent to a compass; and to Darwin it was the one talent without which his stores of knowledge would have been no more than a heap of unclassified specimens in a museum cellar. Moral and physical qualities he had, besides; his patience and his practiced vision were invaluable; but it was the intellectual part that penetrated the secrets of nature. This sense of the problem, this eye for the question, was most serviceable to his success. His acuteness in perceiving the importance of the infinitely little, which is often mentioned as one of his distinguishing traits, was only an incident of this larger endowment; and his power to make other men useful to him, specialists in horticulture or physiology, or even common observing men, was only the knowledge of how to put practical questions. The point is worth emphasizing, because in this age of the accumulation of scientific detail it is too apt to be forgotten that the thinking mind is as rare in science as in other departments, and is, nevertheless, the indispensable thing which makes a man great.

Here it is worth while to advert to that persistent discussion respecting the nature of a modern education, which Darwin's experience is bound to bring forward with renewed vigor. His testimony, both in the chart of himself which he gave Mr. Galton and in the account he wrote for his children, is unequivocal. He says he was self-taught; that his training at the university was of no use to him, speaking generally; and that the classics in particular were barren. He seems to be quite correct in his statement; the claim that his powers of observation and comparison were really developed by school-boy attention to Latin and Greek terminations is purely pedagogical; nor is there any reason to question that men of genius can be successful, achieve eminent greatness for themselves, and do work of the highest value to society without immediate obligation to those studies usually called the humanities. This is nothing new. Instances of self-education for special careers are to be found in other walks than those of science : in war, in administration, and generally in active life, and not infrequently in literature itself. But it is worth observing what testimony these volumes bear to the wonderful vitality of the Greek intelligence. Speaking of the theory of Pangenesis, Darwin writes to a correspondent that the views of Hippocrates " seem almost identical with mine, — merely a change of terms, and an application of them to classes of facts necessarily unknown to the old philosopher." Again, he writes of Aristotle : " From quotations which I had seen I had a high notion of Aristotle's merits, but I had not the most remote notion what a wonderful man he was. Linnæus and Cuvier have been my two gods, though in very different ways, but they were mere schoolboys to old Aristotle. . . . I never realized, before reading your book, to what an enormous consummation of labor we owe even our common knowledge." A more striking passage is that of Huxley's, where he says : " The oldest of all philosophies, that of evolution, was bound hand and foot and cast into utter darkness during the millennium of theological scholasticism. But Darwin poured new life-blood into the ancient frame; the bonds burst, and the revivified thought of ancient Greece has proved itself to be a more adequate expression of the universal order of things than any of the schemes which have been accepted by the credulity and welcomed by the superstition of seventy later generations of men." Rediscovery, however, is not obligation; and, perhaps, if Darwin had been thoroughly imbued with the Greek mode of looking upon the universe, he would not have been really indebted to it for his own views; for he went upon different grounds in forming his conceptions. The real question is, not whether Darwin succeeded without Greek influences, but whether he lost anything because of his failure to assimilate them. The answer seems plain. It is written all over these pages, and is expressly given by Darwin in more than one passage.

No words can be too strong to express the lovableness of Darwin's personality, or the moral beauty of his character. In his biography, it is true, he is presented as the man of science; but he is seen occasionally in other aspects. He was a dutiful, respectful, and affectionate son, at the outset of his life. He thought his father was sometimes unjust, but he always spoke of him as "the wisest man he ever knew;" and there is a touching passage in one of his letters home, when his father had sent him a note: "I almost cried for pleasure at receiving it; it was very kind, thinking of writing to me." He was also, in his turn, an admirable father, considerate, patient, and very tender. One of his sons tells a most significant anecdote of once having drawn on himself some indignant exclamation, "almost with fury," and the end of it being that "next morning, at seven o'clock or so, he came into my bedroom and sat on my bed, and said he had not been able to sleep, from the thought that he had been so angry with me, and after a few more kind words he left me." His description of his little daughter who died is of itself enough to show the extraordinarily fine quality of his affections; and in general his relations with his children are almost ideal in gentleness, kindness, and companionableness. He was also a good friend and acquaintance. In a word, in his private social relations he was exemplary, judged by the standard of a high civilization. He was not without a sense, too, of public duty.

He felt strongly only upon the subject of slavery, and this was largely because of his travels in slave countries. He was interested in philanthropic efforts to some degree, and especially in furthering the increase of kindness to animals. But he was remote from public affairs, and led even in his sympathies a life somewhat narrowly confined to his own circle and his work in science. In other parts of his character there is nothing to displease. He was modest and just, and free from envy, conscientious to an extreme, and as ready to give as to receive help in all ways. He was more pleased with his fame than he acknowledged; he cared deeply for the success of his theory, and was well aware of its influence on his own reputation as one to be classed with Newton's; he liked praise and distinction, though he limited his desire to the commendation and respect of naturalists; but this is only to wish to be approved by the most competent judges. He was fair to Wallace, and exhibited the best of tempers toward him; but between the lines one reads that he was nettled and annoyed by the incident, and it must be concluded that as he was ambitious in youth, he was desirous of having his due in manhood, and valued fame.

This was a character which might well spare the humanities. The fact remains that he did spare them. What he lost was culture. The confession that he makes of the gradual atrophy of his æsthetic tastes will be long quoted as one of the most remarkable facts of his life. He began with a susceptibility to music, which by his son's account he did not lose; with a liking for poetry, such that he read The Excursion twice, and he would not have read it except for pleasure; and he used to take Milton with him in his pocket. In art he went but a little way, if, indeed, he ever really had any eye for it. He was religious, as an English boy usually is; but his interest in belief regarding religious subjects died out, and, what is of more consequence, the emotions which were called out by it in early life ceased to be exercised. There was a deadening, in other words, of all his nature, except so far as it was fed by his work, his family, and his friends in its intellectual and social parts. So complete was this change that it affected even his appreciation of beautiful scenery, which had evidently given him keen delight in his youth and travels. He dates this change from just after his thirtieth year, when he became absorbed in scientific pursuits as his profession. Something, no doubt, and perhaps much, is to be set down to the effect of his ill-health, which left him with diminished energies for any recreation; his strength was exhausted in his few hours of work. He was himself so convinced that his life had been narrowed in these ways, that he says if he had it to live over he would have planned to give a certain time habitually to poetry.

It would be too much to say that the failure of Darwin to appropriate the humane elements in his university education accounts in any perceptible degree for these defects. In culture, as in science, the self-making power of the man counts heavily; and there is such inefficiency in those whose duty it is to give youth a liberal education from classical sources, there are such wrong methods and unintelligent aims in the universities, that it might easily prove to be the case that a student with the most cordial temperament toward the humanities would profit only imperfectly by his residence at seats of learning. In spite of these reservations however, the Greek culture is the historical source of what are traditionally the higher elements in our intellectual life, and has been for most cultivated men the practical discipline of their minds. But it is to be further observed that the example of Darwin, if it should be set up as showing that Greek culture is unnecessary in modern days, goes just as directly and completely to prove that all literary education, as well by modern as by ancient authors, is superfluous. It is enough to indicate to what a length the argument must be carried, if it is at all admitted. The important matter is rather the question, How much was Darwin's life injured for himself by his loss of culture, in the fact that some of those sources of intellectual delight which are reputed the most precious for civilized man were closed to him ?

The blank page in this charming biography is the page of spiritual life. There is nothing written there. The entire absence of an element which enters commonly into all men's lives in some degree is a circumstance as significant as it is astonishing. Never was a man more alive to what is visible and tangible, or in any way matter of sensation; on the sides of his nature where an appeal could be made, never was a man more responsive; but there were parts in which he was blind and dull. Just as the boy failed to be interested in many things, the man failed too; and he disregarded what did not interest him with the same ease at sixty as at twenty. What did interest him was the immediately present, and he dealt with it admirably, both in the intellectual and the moral world; but what was remote was as if it were not. The spiritual element in life is not remote, but it is not matter of sensation, and Darwin lived as if there were no such thing; it belongs to the region of emotion and imagination, and those perceptions which deal with the nature of man in its contrast with the material world. Poetry, art, music, the emotional influences of nature, the idealizations of moral life, are the means by which men take possession of this inner world of man; to which, for man at least, nature in all its immensity is subsidiary. Darwin's insensibility to the higher life — for so men agree to call it — was partly, if not wholly, induced by his absorption in scientific pursuits in the spirit of materialism. We praise him for his achievements, we admire his character, and we feel the full charm of his temperament; he delights us in every active manifestation of his nature. We do not now learn for the first time that a man may be good without being religious, and successful without being liberally educated, and worthy of honor without being spiritual; but a man may be all this and yet be incomplete. Great as Darwin was as a thinker, and winning as he remains as a man, those elements in which he was deficient are the noblest part of our nature.

BYRON'S CENTENARY.

THE absence of any widespread interest in the centenary of Lord Byron is a marvelous illustration of the vicissitudes of literary reputation. Only in Greece was public notice taken of it. The brilliancy with which his fame burst forth, the unexampled rapidity with which it spread through Europe, the powerful influence it continued to exert on the youth of the next age, were to the men who witnessed them sure signs of the magnitude of his future renown. The decadence into which it has fallen would have been incredible to them. It was Byron's distinction to have been the first man of letters who enjoyed an international reputation at once; and one can hardly credit the fact that he has shrunk so wonderfully. In the month of his death Sir Walter Scott, in a brief article which attracted wide attention, said that it seemed almost as if the sun in heaven had been extinguished; and when Scott soon followed him, Landor, writing to

Crabb Robinson, remarked that the death of these two had " put the fashionable world into deep mourning," and drew gloomy predictions, in the well-known manner of contemporaries, because the great men were leaving no successors.

Something of the shock of Byron's death and of the exaltation of his genius at the moment was due to the manner in which he met his end; he had fallen like one of his own heroes, died in a cause, and appealed to the romantic feeling of the age. Even then, however, to admire him was found to be a different thing from approving him. When the thirty-seven guns had been fired at Missolonghi, and the Turks had responded with " an exultant volley," and the ship had brought home the remains, the Abbey was refused, and he was buried in the common soil of England. Two incidents of the funeral bring him very near to us. Lady Caroline Lamb met the cortège as she was driving, and, on being told, in answer to her question, that it was Byron's, fainted in her carriage; and Mary Shelley, as she saw the procession winding down, reflected · on the short-sightedness of human life, asking who could have foretold at Lerici such changes as she had witnessed in two little years.

Hobhouse, with all his efforts, could raise only a thousand pounds for a memorial, but with this he got Thorwaldsen to make a statue which was sent to England in 1834. The Abbey was again refused, and, to the discredit of the nation, this work was allowed to remain stored away in the Custom-house eleven years, because no fit place could be got to put it in. At last, in 1845, Dr. Whewell gave permission to set it up in the Library of Trinity, which it still adorns. Thirty years later came the miserable fiasco of Beaconsfield's Committee, which, far from making Newstead Abbey a national possession and gathering there the relics of Byron, placed in Hamilton Park (other sites being refused) that statue of the poet leaning on the rocks, with his dog Boatswain beside him, which can only be described as popular melodrama in stone, beautiful only for the mass of red marble which the Greek Government gave for its base. It is to be remarked, also, that at this time the Abbey was a third time practically refused, as Dean Stanley, out of respect to the action of his two predecessors, but not apparently for any other reason, precluded application for erecting a tablet there by a letter in which he said he preferred the subject should not be brought before him.

The history of monuments, however, is not necessarily proof of fame. Others of England's greatest do not sleep in the Abbey, and the hero not infrequently waits for his statue a long age. The place of fame is on the lips of men, and Macaulay, when Moore's Life came out, could speak of Byron as " the most celebrated man in Europe." The decline of his vogue was nevertheless rapid and unmistakable. We all remember Carlyle's oracle : " Close . thy Byron ; open thy Goethe." This must have been about 1840. But, unfortunately, as one writer observes, to open Goethe is to return to Byron's greatness. Did not Goethe tell Eckermann that a man of Byron's eminence would not come again, nor such a tragedy as Cain ? He thought him greater than Milton — " vast and widely varied," whereas the latter was only simple and stately. Perhaps, as we have been told, Goethe was flattered by Byron's imitation.

Whatever was the reason, the critical judgment of Goethe is one to be weighed with regard to Byron, and to himself also, for that matter. What part Goethe's praise may have had in making Byron the hero of "Young Germany" we have no means of determining, but his works were vital in the new age there, and still his hold seems greater on the Germans, if we may judge by the test of translations and biography, than it is elsewhere on the Continent. Heine was more than touched by him, though he was far from being his duplicate, and could see the humorous side of those young Parisians — Musset the foremost — who were melancholy in the full glow of first manhood, and went about in despair dining sumptuously every day. One pities Musset, for Byron was, as much as another man can be, the secret of his fate. Lamartine caught only the sentimentality of Byron, but Musset assimilated his darker spirit, his recklessness, and license, and skepticism, and transmuted his very coarseness into a Parisian vulgarity. Stendhal and Sainte-Beuve paid tribute to him; and, to cut the subject short, Mazzini thanked him in the name of Italy, in Spain Espronceda drew his inspiration from him, and Castelar, in the later time, eulogized him for his liberating influences in the peninsula with Spanish amplitude of phrase. Karl Elze thinks that the Russian poet,

Pushkin, was his child; if it were so, Byron might well be proud of what such an influence was the beginning of in Russia. This rapid survey, with its brilliant names, impresses the mind with the range and dominance of this man, although Landor's sneer, when he hoped that "the mercies which have begun with man's forgetfulness may be crowned with God's forgiveness," does not now seem so absurd as formerly.

To look at the matter from this point of view, however, is to confuse Byron with Byronism. There was a European mood, a temperament of the revolutionary time, that fed on Byron, but he was not its creator, and to regard him as more than a single influence of many that moulded the young men of the next generation is to give him vastly more than his due. This is the secret of his vogue in Europe, not that he liberated their minds, but that he set the fashion for minds expanding in a new age of intellectual pride and moral irresponsibility, helped to form their attitude, and was a rallying name for the faction. He was licentious, but he was neither democratical nor atheistical; he had no body of opinions properly thought out and correlated with social facts, either in politics or religion; he had no strong convictions even; but, with prejudices of rank and reminiscences of Scottish theology from which he could not free himself, he was an impulsive and therefore uneven revolter from the old régime, and never quite at home in the new camp. He preferred, he said, to be beheaded by the King and not by the mob; and the whole aristocrat spoke in the saying. Shelley wrote of him, " The canker of aristocracy needs to be cut out;" and he hits off Byron's inconsequence in religion where he speaks of him under the name of Maddalo, and contrasts him with himself. Maddalo, he says, took a wicked pleasure in drawing out his taunts against religion; but, he adds, " What Maddalo thinks on these matters is not exactly known." Byron is believed to have talked with Shelley more seriously than with any other man. He did not himself know what he thought; and his state of mind was well expressed by his remark to Lady Byron, " The trouble is, I *do* believe." In substance, therefore, unlike Shelley, who was democratical and atheistical on principle, Byron was far from being the ideal of the various " young " nationalities,

France, Germany, Italy, and Spain, in the principal tenets dear to the age. It was rather his personality, and what they transformed him into by their worship, that had power over them in their search for "liberty;" and truly, though his ideas were incomplete and fragmentary, and inextricably blended, even in their formation, with his impulses and the accidents of his position as a pariah of genius, yet there was a contagion in his spirit, a dash of energy and of abandon, that told as blood tells more than thought.

One advantage, too, Byron had with foreign nations that with his own counts as a defect. He had no form, no art, no finish; and the poet who failed in these things can be read in our day only by a kind of sufferance, and with continual friction with what has come to be our mastering literary taste for perfection in the manner. It has been said that he consequently bore translation better than he otherwise would. His quality is power, not charm; the mood and the situation and the thought are the elements that count in his poetry, while the words are at the best eloquent or witty, but not " the living garment of light." The result was, that he could be given almost completely in a foreign language. This consideration may go far to explain the relative estimate of him by foreign writers in comparison with other English poets; for these others who have the charm that cannot be transfused, the art that will obey no master but its own Prospero, are seen, as one may say, without their singing robes; and their poetry, made prose, loses half its excellence. This, together with the German element in one portion of his work and the strong Italian influence in a larger portion, especially in Don Juan, must be taken into account in any attempt to understand why he was the best known English poet on the Continent, and perhaps, with the exception of Shakespeare, still is.

In England, Byron's reputation met with rapid decline from natural causes. It is not likely that his misconduct in morals was much against him, and Beaconsfield was wholly on the wrong track when he reminded the Byron meeting that, after half a century, a man's private life scarcely enters into the estimate of his literary genius. It seems rather Byron's lack of orthodoxy that England most resented. Society put up with much libertinism in those days in high quarters ; but Byron had attacked the faith, or at least elements of it, which the Church shared in common with Calvinism, and this was too shocking a matter for a society which found hardly more than matter for gossip in natural sons and daughters. This was the reason which a bishop alleged in the House of Lords in answer to Brougham, in the debate on the second refusal of the Abbey. Byron had attacked Christianity, and he should not be interred " in the Temple of our God." The middle classes have always rejected Byron, in like manner, because he scoffed, though, no doubt, his life and the licentious portions of his poetry also offended them. From the first his skepticism was heavily against him, and probably it still remains the strongest objection to his works in the minds of Englishmen generally. In Landor's bitter attack (he had offended Landor by rhyming his name with *gander*) this charge is made the climax, and the passage is brief enough to quote as the best word of Byron's enemies : —

" Afterwards, whenever he wrote a bad poem, he supported his sinking fame by some signal act of profligacy: an elegy by a seduction, a heroic by an adultery, a tragedy by a divorce. On the remark of a learned man that irregularity is no indication of genius, he began to lose ground rapidly, when, on a sudden, he cried out at the Haymarket, *There is no God.* It was then surmised more generally and more gravely that there was something in him, and he stood upon his legs almost to the last. Say what you will, once whispered a friend of mine, there are things in him strong as poison and original as sin." This, with all its excess, is no inapt character of Byron, as English prejudice drew him.

On the other hand, much that was in his favor at first was necessarily temporary. The man had a story. He was one of the picturesque characters of the age, and while he lived he was interesting to his time merely for his personal fortunes. It was to his gain, too, that he identified his own romance with that which he early invented, appealing to the adventurous in men and to the pity and admiration of women. His heroes are strong, and strength succeeds with the sex in fiction as well as in life ; and they are, besides, usually faithful in love, while their crimes are taken out of the moral region of deliberate choice by a kind of emo-

tional sophistry, and somehow are charged
to their circumstances, so that the unwary
and innocent reader commiserates their vil-
lainies instead of being revolted by them.
These tales (and no part of his work was
more popular) are hard to read to-day, but
we forget too readily what raw and bloody
fiction the world had in the first score years
of this century; we cannot conceive how
London ran after stories of blighted brig-
ands and sentimental corsairs, in the very
thunder of Waterloo. But so it was, and
Byron was more interesting in that he was
the unhappy and noble original from which
the pirates of his imagination were drawn.
If he changed the scene and wandered over
Europe as Childe Harold, he gained in sentiment; if he wore the mask of Manfred, he
gained in tragedy; and if he sneered in Don
Juan, there was the jaded man of the world,
perhaps more interesting. He was, moreover, a peer; but a dead peer certainly is
no better than a dead lion, and when he
died, why, — the fashion in collars changed.
Other living personalities occupied the stage;
England grew steadily more sincere in religion, more strict in the standard of private morals, more exacting of seriousness in

thought and of perfection in literary form; and all these influences were adverse to Byron, who made no offsetting gain in his own country from the revolutionary fervor that helped him on the Continent.

What is there left? Some stirring passages of adventure, some eloquent descriptions of nature, some personal lyrics of true poetic feeling, dramas which, it is to be hoped, have finally damned "the unities," and one great poem of the modern spirit, Don Juan. And what remains of that melodramatic Byron of women's fancies? His character has come out plain, and we are really amazed at it, — proud, sensual, selfish, and, it must be added, mean. Ignoble he was, in many ways, but, for all that, the energy of his passions, his vitality, his masterly egotism, and the splendid force of his genius, made him a commanding name and stamped him upon the succeeding European time. He cannot be neglected by history, but men certainly appear to pass him by. Arnold has endeavored to bring him back by a collection; but Arnold's critical views on poetry seem to be justifications in age for the tastes he had when he was young, — reasons after the act. A late biographer thinks that the decadence of his fame is due to the conservatism of the last half-century, and that in the revolutionary age that ought soon to be beginning, he will retrieve himself. But can this be hoped of a " revolutionary " poet whom Swinburne has cast aside? The prediction does not convince us. Byronism has gone by, and the age of the " enlightenment " in Germany and France; such a mood is not repeated. Goethe outlived Wertherism, but had Byron such good fortune? In his own character there are such defects as forbid admiration in the light of our moral ideas; and in his poems, taken apart from their time, there are other defects, both in their substance, and, unquestionably, in their form, which forbid the sort of approval that would make them in a true sense classic, as a whole, though the qualities that make Childe Harold and Don Juan great, and preserve here and there passages in other poems, are those that confer immortality. He was a poet; he was a force, also, that spent itself partly in creating a world-wide affectation, and partly in rousing and reinforcing the impulse of individual liberty on the Continent; but he is a poet no one can love, and he left a memory that no one can admire, and there is none of his works that receives the meed of perfect praise. And, as to the fruits of that vast influence, is it hard to say whether they were more good than evil?

ON BROWNING'S DEATH.

THE death of Browning brings one stage nearer the too plainly approaching end of a literary age which will long be full of curious interest to the student of the moods of the mind of man. Time has linked his name with that of Tennyson, and the conjunction gives to England another of those double stars of genius in which her years are rich, and by which the spirit of an age has a two-fold expression. The old opposition, the polarity of mind, by virtue of which the Platonist differs from the Aristotelian, the artist from the thinker, Shakespeare from Jonson, shows its efficacy here, too, in the last modern age, and divides the poets and their admirers by innate preferences. It is needful to remember this contrast, though not to insist upon it unduly, in order to approach the work of Browning rightly, to be just to those who idolize him without offense to those who are repelled by him. The analysis of his powers, the charting of his

life and work, are not difficult; but the
value of his real achievement is more uncer-
tain. Interest centres entirely in his poetry,
for his career has been without notable incident, and is told when it is said that he has
lived the life of a scholar and man of letters
in England and Italy amid the social culture of his time. For the world, his career
is the succession of books he has put forth,
and this is as he would have it; publicity
beyond this he did not seek, but refused
with violence and acrimony.

In his earliest poem, youthful in its self-
portraiture, its literary touch, and its fragmentary plan, the one striking quality is the flow
of language. Here was a writer who would
never lack for words; fluent, as if inexhaustible, the merely verbal element in Pauline
shows no struggle with the medium of the
poet's art. This gift of facility was, as is
usual, first to show itself. In Paracelsus
the second primary quality of Browning was
equally conspicuous, — the power of reasoning in verse. These two traits have for a
poet as much weakness as strength, and they
lie at the source of Browning's defects as
a master of poetic art. His facility allowed
him to be diffuse in language, and his rea-

soning habit led him often to be diffuse in matter. In Sordello the two produced a monstrosity, both in construction and expression, not to be rivaled in literature. Picturesque detail, intellectual interest, moral meaning, struggle in vain in that tale to make themselves felt and discerned through the tangle of words and the labyrinth of act and reflection. But already in these poems Browning had shown, to himself, if not to the world, that he had come to certain conclusions, to a conception of human life and a decision as to the use of his art in regard to it, which were to give him substantial power. He defined it by his absorption in Paracelsus with the broad ideas of infinite power and infinite love, which in his last poem still maintain their place in his system as the highest solvents of experience and speculation; and in Sordello he stated the end of art, which he continued to seek, in his maxim that little else is worth study except the " history of a soul." His entire poetic work, broadly speaking, is the illustration of this short sentence. Such prepossessions with the spiritual meaning of life as these poems show made sure the predominance in his work of the higher interests of man; and he won his audience finally by this fact, that he had something to say that was ethical and religious. The development, however, of both the theory and practice of his mind had to be realized in far more definite and striking forms than the earlier poems before the attention of the world could be secured.

It would seem natural that a man with such convictions as Browning acknowledged, should be preëminently an idealist, and that his point of weakness should prove to be the tendency to metaphysical and vague matter not easily putting on poetical form. But he was, in fact, a realist, — one who is primarily concerned with things, and uses the method of observation. His sense for actual fact is always keen. In that poem of Paracelsus, which is a discussion in the air if ever a poem was, it is significant to find him emphasizing the circumstance that he had taken very few liberties with his subject, and bringing books to show evidence of historical fidelity. But, little of the dramatic spirit as there is in Paracelsus, there was much in Browning when it should come to be released, and it belongs to the dramatist to be interested in the facts of life, the flesh and blood reality, in which he may or may not (according to his greatness) find a soul. Browning was thus a realist, and he chose habitually the objective method of art — but to set forth "the history of a soul." Had he been an idealist, his subject would have been "the history of *the* soul;" his method might or might not have been different. This change of the particle is a slight one, but it involves that polarity of mind which sets Browning opposite to Tennyson. He deals with individuals, takes in imagination their point of view, assumes for the time being their circumstances and emotions; and one who does this in our time, with a pre-occupation with the soul in the individual, cannot escape from one overpowering impression, repeated from every side of the modern age, — the impression, namely, of the relativity of human life.

This is the lesson which is spread over Browning's pages, with line on line and precept on precept. By it he comes into harmony with the very spirit of the century on its intellectual side, and represents it. The "history of a soul" differs very greatly according to circumstance, native impulses, the needs of life at different stages of growth,

the balance of faculties and desires in it, the
temperament of its historical period, the
access to it of art or music or thought, and
in a thousand ways; and Browning devotes
himself oftentimes to the exposition of all
this web of circumstance, in order that we
may see the soul as it was under its conditions, instead of leaping to a conclusion
by a hard-and-fast morality based upon the
similarity of the soul in all men. The task
happily falls in with his fine gift of reasoning, and increases by practice the supple-
ness and subtlety of this faculty of his. One
might say, indeed, without close computa-
tion, that the larger part of his entire poetic
work is occupied with such reasoning upon
psychological cases, in the manner of a law-
yer who educes a client's justification from
the details of his temptation. Many of the
longer poems are only instances of special
pleading, and have all the faults that belong
to that form of thought. The Ring and the
Book is such an interminable argument, marvelous for intellectual resource, for skill in
dialectic, for plausibility. Bishop Blougram,
Mr. Sludge, Prince Hohenstiel-Schwangau,
and others, readily occur to mind as being
in the same way "apologies;" and in these

7

one feels that, while it is well to know what the prisoner urges on his own behalf, it is the shabby, the cowardly, the criminal, the base, the detestable, that is masking under a too well-woven cloak of words, and that the special pleader is pursuing his game at the risk of a higher honesty than consists in the mere understanding of the mechanism of motive and act. Yet this catholicity, which seems to have for its motto, " Who understands all, forgives all," is a natural consequence in a mind so impressed with the doctrine of the relativity of human life as was Browning's. The tendency of the doctrine is to efface moral judgment, and to substitute for it intellectual comprehension; and usually this results in a practical fatalism, acquiesced in if not actively held. Here, too, Browning's mental temperament has another point of contact with the general spirit of the age, and allows him to take up into his genius the humanitarian instinct so powerful in his contemporaries. For the perception of the excuses for men's action in those of low or morbid or deformed development liberalizes the mind, and the finding of the spark of soul in such individuals does mean to the Christian the finding of that immortal part which equalizes all in an equal destiny, however the difference may look between men while the process of life is going on. Browning came very early to this conviction, that in all men, however weak or grossly set this spark may be, it is to be sought for. In this he is consistently philanthropic and democratic, Christian in spirit and practice, comprehensive in tolerance, large in charity, intellectually (but not emotionally) sympathetic. It is perhaps unnecessary to add that his love of righteousness is not so striking a trait.

But what in all this view of life is most original in Browning is something that possibly perplexes even his devoted admirers. Life, he says, no matter what it may be in its accidents of time, or place, or action, is the stuff to make the soul of. In the humblest as the noblest, in Caliban as in Prospero, the life vouchsafed is the means (adequate, he seems to say, in all cases) of which the soul makes use to grow in. He thus avoids the deadening conclusions to which his doctrine of relativity might lead, by asserting the equal and identical opportunity in all to develop the soul. He unites with

this the original theory — at least one that
he has made his own — that whatever the
soul seeks it should seek with all its might ;
and, pushing to the extreme, he urges that
if a man sin, let him sin to the uttermost of
his desire. This is the moral of the typical
poem of this class, The Statue and the Bust,
and he means more by this than that the
intention, sinning in thought, is equivalent
to sinning in act, — he means that a man
should have his will. No doubt this is
directly in accord with the great value he
places on strength of character, vitality in
life, on resolution, courage, and the braving
of consequences. But the ignoring of the
immense value of restraint as an element in
character is complete ; and in the case of
many whose choice is slowly and doubtfully
made in those younger years when the desire
for life in its fullness of experience is strongest, and the wisdom of knowledge of life in.
its effects is weakest, the advice to obey impulse at all costs, to throw doubt and authority to the winds, and " live my life and
have my day," is of dubious utility. Over
and over again in Browning's poetry one
meets with this insistence on the value of
moments of high excitement, of intense liv-

ing, of full experience of pleasure, even though such moments be of the essence of evil and fruitful in all dark consequences. It is probable that a deep optimism underlies all this; that Browning believed that the soul does not perish in its wrong-doing, but that through this experience, too, as through good, it develops finally its immortal nature, and that, as in his view the life of the soul is in its energy of action, the man must act even evil if he is to grow at all. Optimism, certainly, of the most thorough-going kind this is; but Browning is so consistent an optimist in other parts of his philosophy that this defense may be made for him on a point where the common thought and deepest conviction of the race, in its noblest thinkers and purest artists, are opposed to him, refusing to believe that the doing of evil is to be urged in the interest of true manliness.

The discussion of Browning's attitude towards life in the actual world of men has led away from the direct consideration of the work in which he embodied his convictions. The important portion of it came in middle life, when he obtained mastery of the form of poetic art known as the dramatic monologue. A realist, if he be a poet, must resort to the drama. It was inevitable in Browning's case. Yet the drama, as a form, offered as much unfitness for Browning's genius as it did fitness. The drama requires energy, it is true, and interest in men as individuals; and these Browning had. It also requires concentration, economy of material, and constructive power; and these were difficult to Browning. He did not succeed in his attempts to write drama in its perfect form. He could make fragments of intense power in passion; he could reveal a single character at one critical moment of its career; he could sum up a life history in a long soliloquy; but he could not do more than this and keep the same level of performance. Why he failed is a curious question, and will doubtless be critically debated with a plentiful lack of results. His growth in dramatic faculty, in apprehension of the salient points of character and grasp in presenting them, in perception of the value of situation and power to use it to the full, can readily be traced; but there comes a point where the growth stops. Superior as his mature work is to that of his youth in all these qualities, it falls short of that perfect

and complex design and that informing life
which mark the developed dramatist. In
the monologues he deals with incidents in
a life, with moods of a personality, with the
consciousness which a man has of his own
character at the end of his career; but he
seizes these singly, and at one moment. His
characters do not develop before the eye;
he does not catch the soul in the very act;
he does not present life so much as the results of life. He frequently works by the
method of retrospect, he tells the story, but
does not enact it. In all these he displays
the governing motive of his art, which is to
reveal the soul; but if the soul reveals itself
in his verses, it is commonly by confession,
not presentation. He has, in fact, that
malady of thought which interferes with the
dramatist's control of his hand; he is thinking *about* his characters, and only indirectly
in them, and he is most anxious to convey
his reflections upon the psychical phenom-
enon which he is attending to. In other
words, he is, primarily, a moralist; he reasons, and he is fluent in words and fertile in
thoughts, and so he loses the object itself,
becomes indirect, full of afterthought and
parenthesis, and impairs the dramatic effect.

These traits may be observed, in different degrees, in many of the poems, even in the best. In the dramas themselves the lack of constructive power is absolute. Pippa Passes is only a succession of dramatic fragments artificially bound together, and in the others the lack of body and interdependent life between the parts is patent to all. In a Balcony, certainly one of his finest wrought poems, is only an incident. He is at his best when his field is most narrow — in such a poem as The Laboratory.

There is a compensation for these deficiencies of power in that the preference of his mind for a single passion or mood or crisis at its main moment opens to him the plain and unobstructed way to lyrical expression. His dramatic feeling of the passion and the situation supplies an intensity which finds its natural course in lyrical exaltation. It may well be thought, if it were deemed necessary to decide upon the best in Browning's work, that his genius is most nobly manifest in those lyrics and romances which he called dramatic. The scale rises from his argumentative and moralizing verse, however employed, through those monologues which obey the necessity for greater concen-

tration as the dramatic element enters into
them, up to those most powerful and direct
poems in which the intensity of feeling en-
forces a lyrical movement and lift; and
akin to these last are the songs of love or heroism into which the dramatic element does
not enter. Indeed, Browning's lyrical gift
was more perfect than his dramatic gift;
he knew the secret of a music which has
witchery in it independent of what the words
may say, and when his hand fell on that
chord, he mastered the heart with real poetic
charm. It was seldom, however, that this
happy moment came to him, ennobling his
language and giving wing to his emotion;
and, such poems being rare, it remains true
that the best of his work is to be sought in
those pieces, comprehending more of life,
where his dramatic power takes on a lyrical
measure. Such work became more infre-
quent as years went on, and he declined
again into that earlier style of wordy ratioci-
nation, of tedious pleading as of a lawsuit,
of mere intellectuality as of the old hair-
splitting schoolmen, though he retained the
strength and definiteness of mind which mere
growth had brought to him, and he occasionally produced a poem which was only less

good than the best of his middle age. The translations from the Greek with which he employed his age stand in a different class from his original poems, and were a fortunate resort for his vigorous but now feebly creative mind. At the end he still applied himself to the interpretation of individual lives, but in choosing them he was attracted even more uniformly by something exceptional, often grotesque, in them, and hence they are more curious and less instructive than the earlier work of the same kind.

The mass of Browning's writings which has been glanced at as the expression of the reasoning, the dramatic, or the lyrical impulse in his genius has attracted attention as wide as the English language, and it has been intimated that this success has been won in some degree on other than poetic grounds. It is fair to say, in view of the facts, that many who have felt his appeal to them have found a teacher rather than a poet. Two points in which he reflects his age have been mentioned, but there is a third point which has perhaps been more efficacious than his sense of the relativity of human life or his conviction of the worth of every human soul: he adds to these cardinal doctrines a firm and loudly asseverated religious belief. It is the more noteworthy because his reasoning faculty might in his time have led him almost anywhere rather than to the supreme validity of truth arrived at by intuition. This makes his character the more interesting, for the rationalizing mind which submits itself to intuitive faith exactly parallels in Browning the realist with a predominating interest in the soul. There is no true contradiction in this, no inconsistency; but the combination is unusual. It is natural that, in a time of decreasing authority in formal religion, a poet in Browning's position should wield an immense attraction, and owe something, as Carlyle did, to the wish of his audience to be reassured in their religious faith. Browning had begun with that resolution of the universe into infinite power and infinite love of which something has already been said, and he continued to teach that through nature we arrive at the conception of omnipotence, and through the soul at the conception of love, and he apparently finds the act of faith in the belief that infinite power will finally be discerned as the instrument and expression of infinite love. This is pure optimism; and

in accordance with it he preaches his gospel,
which is that each soul should grow to its
utmost in power and in love, and in the face
of difficulties — of mysteries in experience
or thought — should repose with entire trust
on the doctrine that God has ordered life
beneficently, and that we who live should
wait with patience, even in the wreck of our
own or others' lives, for the disclosure here-
after which shall reconcile to our eyes and
hearts the jar with justice and goodness of
all that has gone before. This is a system
simple enough and complete enough to live
by, if it be truly accepted. It is probable,
however, that Browning wins less by these
doctrines, which are old and commonplace,
than by the vigor with which he dogmatizes
upon them; the certainty with which he
speaks of such high matters; the fervor, and
sometimes the eloquence, with which, touching on the deepest and most secret chords of
the heart's desire, he strikes out the notes of
courage, of hope and vision, and of the fore-
tasted triumph. The energy of his own faith
carries others along with it; the manliness
of his own soul infects others with its cheer
and its delight in the struggle of spiritual
life on earth; and all this the more because

he is learned in the wisdom of the Rabbis, is conversant with modern life and knowledge in all its range, is gifted with intellectual genius, and yet displays a faith the more robust because it is not cloistered, the more credible because it is not professional.

The character of Browning's genius, his individual traits, the general substance of his thought, do not admit of material misconception. It is when the question is raised upon the permanent value of his work that the opportunity for wide divergence arises. That there are dreary wastes in it cannot be gainsaid. Much is now unreadable that was excused in a contemporary book; much never was readable at all; and of the remainder how much will the next age in its turn cast aside? Its serious claim to our attention on ethical, religious, or intellectual grounds may be admitted, without pledging the twentieth century, which will have its own special phases of thought, and thinkers to illustrate them. Browning must live, as the other immortals do, by the poetry in him. It is true he has enlarged the field of poetry by annexing the experience that belongs to the artist and the musician, and has made some of his finest and most original poems out of such motives; and his wide knowledge has served him in other ways, though it has stiffened many a page with pedantry and antiquarianism. It is true that there is a grotesque quality in some of his work, but his humor in this kind is really a pretense; no one laughs at it; it arouses only an amazed wonder, like the stone masks of some mediæval church. In all that he derived from learning and scholarship there is the alloy of mortality; in all his moralizing and special pleading and superfine reasoning there enters the chance that the world may lose interest in his treatment of the subject; in all, except where he sings from the heart itself or pictures life directly and without comment save of the briefest, there is some opportunity for time to breed decay. The faith he preached was the poetical complement of Carlyle's prose, and proceeded from much the same grounds and by the same steps: believe in God, and act like a man — that was the substance of it. But Carlyle himself already grows old and harsh. The class of mind to which Browning belongs depends on its matter for its life; unless he has transformed it into poetry, time will deal hardly with it.

To come to the question which cannot be honestly set aside, although it is no longer profitable to discuss it, Browning has not cared for that poetic form which bestows perennial charm, or else he was incapable of it. He fails in beauty, in concentration of interest, in economy of language, in selection of the best from the common treasure of experience. In those works where he has been most indifferent, as in the Red Cotton Night-Cap Country, he has been merely whimsical and dull; in those works where the genius he possessed is most felt, as in Saul, A Toccata of Galuppi's, Rabbi Ben Ezra, The Flight of the Duchess, The Bishop Orders his Tomb in St. Praxed's Church, Hervé Riel, Cavalier Tunes, Time's Revenges, and many more, he achieves beauty or nobility or fitness of phrase such as only a poet is capable of. It is in these last pieces and their like that his fame lies for the future. It was his lot to be strong as the thinker, the moralist with "the accomplishment of verse," the scholar interested to rebuild the past of experience, the teacher with an explicit dogma to enforce in an intellectual form with examples from life, the anatomist of human passions, instincts, and impulses in all their gamut, the commentator on his own age; he was weak as the artist, and indulged, often unnecessarily and by choice, in the repulsive form — in the awkward, the obscure, the ugly. He belongs with Jonson, with Dryden, with the heirs of the masculine intellect, the men of power not unvisited by grace, but in whom mind is predominant. Upon the work of such poets time hesitates, conscious of their mental greatness, but also of their imperfect art, their heterogeneous matter; at last the good is sifted from that whence worth has departed.